Law Essentials

CONTRACT LAW

D0177389

Law Essentials

CONTRACT LAW

Tikus Little, LL.B.(Hons.), Dip.L.P.

Solicitor;
Teaching Fellow, University of Stirling

DUNDEE UNIVERSITY PRESS
2006

First published in Great Britain in 2006 by
Dundee University Press
University of Dundee
Dundee DD1 4HN

www.dundee.ac.uk/dup

ISBN 1–84586–002–0
EAN 978–1–84586–002–8

No natural forests were destroyed to make this product;
only farmed timber was used and replanted.

British Library Cataloguing-in-Publication Data
A catalogue record for this book is available on request from the British Library

Typeset by Waverley Typesetters, Little Walsingham, Norfolk
Printed and bound by Bell & Bain Ltd, Glasgow

CONTENTS

TABLE OF CASES

TABLE OF STATUTES

1 OVERVIEW AND DEFINITIONS

The law of contract forms the basis of our civil society. Without the law of contract, we could not buy food, clothing or a place to live. We could not secure employment or book a holiday. Businesses could not buy raw materials, hire a workforce or distribute their goods to retailers on the High Street without contracts. Builders would not be obliged to finish building houses. Footballers could flit from club to club on a weekly basis and the purchase of a ticket to see a film would not entitle you to see it. Chaos would reign if the law of contract did not provide a set of legal rules to regulate many aspects of our day-to-day lives.

The law of contract is complex and intricate and disputes over contracts have led to a wealth of court cases over the years. The aim of this book is to give a clear and concise guide to the basics of the law of contract.

OVERVIEW

The key to learning and understanding the law of contract is knowing how it all fits together. Although it has to be taught topic by topic, the successful student should be able to review the law of contract at the end of the course and see "the big picture". Applying contract law to a problem question, in particular, can be difficult as so many legal issues can arise out of one scenario. It is useful, therefore, to begin the study of contract by spending a little time thinking about the big picture. Much of the law interconnects and cannot be learned in isolation. There are a number of important questions to answer when studying contract law and this book sets out to answer those questions.

Does a contract exist?

There are two key issues to consider here: first, not all obligations fall into the category of "contract" and so it is necessary to define those which do; and second, the mechanics of forming a contract are important because a contract imposes legal obligations on the parties to it and so we need to know when those obligations have been formed. These matters will be discussed in Chapters 1: Overview and Definitions; and 2: Formation of Contract.

Can the contract, or any particular term in it, be enforced?

One common misconception in the study of contract law is that the formation of the contract is the end of the story; the parties have entered into an agreement and so must comply with its terms no matter what those terms are or what the circumstances were at the time the contract was made. This is not true. While it is true that most contracts are indeed valid and binding, there are a number of problems with contracts which can affect whether they are valid or not. These problems are discussed in Chapter 3: Problems with Contracts which is divided into eight parts:

(1) Lack of consensus.
(2) Lack of consent.
(3) Lack of capacity.
(4) Lack of formality where required.
(5) Illegality.
(6) Restrictions on the freedom to contract.
(7) Error (misunderstandings and misrepresentation).
(8) Other circumstances surrounding the making of the contract which prejudice it.

What is in the contract and who has rights under it?

Contracts are made up of contractual terms, some of which are express and some of which are implied. It is important to know which terms are included in a contract and which are not because those that are not included are not enforceable as contractual terms (this is called "incorporation"). It is also important to know the effect of certain terms in a contract and so a definition of terms is necessary. It is also necessary to know the rules which the courts will apply in interpreting contracts where the parties are in dispute about what the contract means (this is called "construction"). Finally, we need to know who has rights and obligations under the contract. These matters are discussed in Chapters 4: Contractual Terms and 5: Third Party Rights.

What happens when things go wrong between the parties?

One of the most important areas of contract law concerns breach of contract. This happens when one of the parties does not perform their part of the contract in some way. The key issues of identifying breach of contract and the remedies for breach of contract are discussed in Chapter 6: Breach of Contract.

When does a contract come to an end?

Contracts do not last forever but there are many ways in which a contract can come to an end and these are discussed in Chapter 7: Termination of Contract.

What happens if the parties to the contract live or work in different countries?

Businesses carry out more and more of their business abroad nowadays and the creation of the single market and development of e-commerce means that a lot of this business is now done in the European Union. Students of contract law must know where to find the law on jurisdiction and choice of law when contracts are concluded between parties in different countries and this book will focus on the rules where the parties are within EU Member States. Other rules of international private law will apply to cross-border contracts between the UK and non-EU Member States. The rules are discussed in Chapter 8: Cross-border Contracts.

Reform of the law

Contract law is primarily a common law subject but there is a growing body of legislation which impacts on contract law, particularly where consumers are involved. Some of the developments in contract law are discussed briefly in the Note on Reform.

DEFINITION OF CONTRACT

A good basic definition of a contract is restated in Enid Marshall's *General Principles of Scots Law* which sets out the meaning as "[a]n agreement which creates or is intended to create a legal obligation between the parties to it" (p 221).

The law of contract falls into the category of *voluntary obligations* because the parties must agree to enter into a contract voluntarily; it cannot be imposed upon them. This contrasts with non-voluntary obligations which are imposed by law such as those found in the law of delict.

The contract is therefore an *agreement* based on consensus between the parties.

A contract can also be distinguished from a mere domestic or social arrangement because it must have at its heart the intention to create a *legal obligation* between the parties to it. A legal obligation binds the parties and it is that feature which makes the contract enforceable in law; in other words, parties to a contract must do as it says or face the possibility of being made to comply with its terms through enforcement measures. Some enforcement measures require to be taken in the courts.

When identifying whether or not contracts exist, it is important to establish which category the contract falls into. Voluntary obligations can fall into the following categories in Scots law:

- contract
- promise.

CONTRACT

There are two types of contract, bilateral contracts and gratuitous contracts.

Bilateral contracts

This is the most common type of contract. At its simplest, it has two parties who both have certain obligations under the contract; eg the contract may involve one party paying money in return for goods or services provided by the other party. Buying a loaf of bread, renting a flat and getting on a bus all involve bilateral contracts because both parties have a legally enforceable obligation to do something to fulfil their part of the contract; the landlord must provide the flat in question and the tenant must pay the agreed rent, etc. Most of these contracts are onerous as each party contributes something of financial value to the transaction: money, goods, services, etc.

Gratuitous contracts

A contract between two parties can also be gratuitous because only one of them has obligations under it. This is demonstrated in the case of *Morton's Trustees* v *Aged Christian Friend Society of Scotland* (1899). Mr Morton entered into an arrangement to make charitable donations to the Society subject to certain conditions to be fulfilled by the Society. The Society agreed to Mr Morton's offer to donate money to it on those terms. Payment was to be made by instalments but Mr Morton died before the final two instalments were paid. The Society wanted to enforce the contract which it claimed it had with Mr Morton against his estate to enable it to receive the remaining payments. However, the trustees of his estate disputed that the arrangement was a legally enforceable contract at all. The court held that there was indeed a contract between Mr Morton and the Society under which the final instalments should be paid. It did not matter that the contract did not bestow some sort of consideration or benefit on Mr Morton or his estate – it was still enforceable as a contract.

PROMISE

Promises are also known as "gratuitous unilateral obligations". These are binding in Scots law.

Although most voluntary obligations will fall into the category of onerous bilateral contracts, it is possible under Scots law to have an enforceable obligation which is neither a bilateral contract nor a gratuitous contract. This type of obligation has only one party who can be bound by it (ie unilateral) and is not onerous because it does not impose an obligation on another party to fulfil part of the bargain (ie gratuitous).

The key characteristics of a promise are:

(1) The promisor must intend to be legally bound by his promise.

(2) There is no need for the promisee (the person to whom the promise is made) to accept the promise for it to be binding on the promisor.

(3) Promises can be enforced through the courts by the promisee.

(4) The existence of a promise is difficult to prove: it previously required proof by writ or oath (*Smith* v *Oliver* (1911)) and now requires formal writing, except if given in the course of business (see Chapter 3).

(5) A promise can have conditions attached to it.

Promises can arise in a number of scenarios, as follows.

Business

Promise can be found in a business context in a number of situations:

- Option to buy land: it has been held that granting someone an option to buy land but not putting that in a properly constituted contract could be enforceable by promise (could such an option be enforced as a contract if it were formally written down and agreed between the potential buyer and seller?) (*Stone* v *MacDonald* (1979)).

- A cheque guarantee card is a promise by the bank to honour the cheque.

- Keeping an offer open for a set time has been held to be binding as a promise (*Littlejohn* v *Hadwen* (1882)).

Family arrangements

In the case of *Bathgate* v *Rosie* (1976), a mother promised to pay for repairs to a window broken by her son.

Rewards

Authority for this point is provided by the case of *Petrie* v *Earl of Airlie* (1834) in which the Earl offered a reward to anyone who could identify the person who had published a placard to which the Earl had taken offence. The reward was to be paid on conviction of that person. Petrie named his brother and claimed the reward. The Earl tried to avoid paying by saying that the payment was due only on conviction of the responsible party and, as there was no conviction, there was therefore no need to pay out. The judge decided that conviction was not necessary for the reward to be payable. The Earl was legally obliged to pay the reward, although of course Mr Petrie had never been legally obliged to give the Earl the name of the placard maker.

Although it is difficult to tell the difference between this case and the case of gratuitous contract found in *Morton's Trustees*, the important point to take from this case is that an offer of a reward can be categorised as a promise and can be enforced as such.

English law

The legal classification of promise as a form of obligation which can bind the promisor in law so that he has to make good on that promise contrasts with the position in England which does not accept that a contract can exist without an onerous element; contracts in England must have an element of consideration. This leads English courts to interpret situations which might be classified as "promise" in Scots law as "unilateral contracts", such as the case of *Carlill* v *Carbolic Smoke Ball Co* (1893) in which the "promise" (to pay money to anyone who fell ill after buying and using a smoke ball) contained in a newspaper advert was identified as an offer. (See Chapter 2.) (MacQueen, 1986 SLT (News) 1.)

Frequently Asked Questions

What is the difference between a promise and a gratuitous contract?
The difference between the two is difficult to detect. In general terms, a gratuitous contract arises where A offers to do something for B (usually pay money) *if* B accepts (see Chapter 2 for acceptance). However, if A *promises* B the money then B need not do anything for it to be binding. Unfortunately, this generality is muddied by reward cases like *Petrie* because, of course, the "promise" to pay the reward is only enforceable if the promisee actually does what is asked for in the reward notice (eg name the culprit). Nevertheless,

the reward cases demonstrate that the fact that a promise has conditions attached to it is not, in itself, enough to change it from a promise to a gratuitous contract.

Why do we need to know these classifications?
There are two main reasons why the distinctions are important:

(1) If an arrangement falls into the category of contract or promise then it will be enforceable in law. If it does not, then it will not be enforceable under the law of contract or promise (although it may be covered by other branches of law like unjustified enrichment).

(2) The Requirements of Writing (Scotland) Act 1995 states that certain contracts and obligations must be in writing (see Chapter 3). This Act makes a distinction between "gratuitous unilateral obligations" and "gratuitous contracts". Gratuitous unilateral obligations are promises and *must* be in writing, unless given in the course of business. Gratuitous contracts, on the other hand, do not necessarily have to be in writing.

Essential Facts

- Not all agreements between parties can be categorised as "contracts".
- Voluntary obligations fall into two categories: contract and promise.
- A contract is a voluntary obligation arising out of an agreement between two parties which creates legal obligations between them.
- Contracts fall into two basic categories: (1) bilateral contracts under which each party has rights and obligations which can be enforced; and (2) gratuitous contracts under which only one party has obligations which can be enforced but the other party agrees to it. There must be consent for these contracts to exist.
- Promises are gratuitous unilateral obligations (not requiring the promisee's consent) which can only be enforced by the promisee against the promisor. They are difficult to distinguish from gratuitous contracts because they can have conditions attached to them but the distinction is important because promises, unlike gratuitous contracts, must be in writing to exist (unless given in the course of business). Examples of promise arise in reward cases, options to buy land and cheque guarantee cards.

Essential Cases

Morton's Trustees v Aged Christian Friend Society of Scotland (1899): example of a gratuitous contract.

Stone v MacDonald (1979): example of promise in business (option granted over land in favour of another).

Littlejohn v Hadwen (1882): example of promise in business (keeping an offer open).

Bathgate v Rosie (1976): mother's promise to pay for damage caused by child.

Petrie v Earl of Airlie (1834): reward case = promise

Carlill v Carbolic Smoke Ball Co (1893): English case demonstrating a unilateral contract under English law.

2 FORMATION OF CONTRACT

Formation concerns the process by which contracts are created. Formation of contract is not about the format of the contract (ie whether it is in writing or not) but whether there can be said to be a contract between the parties at all. Most contracts do not have to be in writing but those that do are dealt with in Chapter 3 under "Lack of formality". This chapter identifies the key steps in the actual formation of the contract.

At its most simple, a contract is made when an *offer* is met with an *acceptance*.

OFFER

Definition

An offer must be capable of acceptance (ie not too vague) and it must be communicated to the other party. Importantly, it must include the intention to be legally bound (an offer to meet up for a drink after work would not qualify). It may be verbal or in writing or in some other form (eg vending machines have been held to "offer" their contents for sale: *Thornton* v *Shoe Lane Parking Ltd* (1971)).

It is perhaps easier to explain what an offer is *not*:

Auctions

The auctioneer does not offer the item for sale – he merely issues an invitation to treat and the bidders make offers. However, if the auctioneer advertises that the auction is to be held *without a reserve price* being set for the item then opinion is divided; but it appears from English case law that this stipulation does turn the auctioneer into the offeror for that transaction (*Warlow* v *Harrison* (1859)).

Section 57(2) of the Sale of Goods Act 1979 applies to certain contracts and it makes clear that, in these cases, the bidder makes the offer and the auctioneer then accepts that offer.

Invitation to treat

An offer is not an invitation to treat. An invitation to treat includes displaying goods in a shop or on a website. This is illustrated by the case of *Fisher* v *Bell* (1960) in which a display of flick-knives was held to be an invitation to treat rather than an offer, ie an expression of willingness to receive an offer which can then be accepted or rejected. This distinction was important from the shopkeeper's point of view as categorisation as an offer would have rendered his display a criminal offence under offensive weapons legislation.

Similarly, the case of *Pharmaceutical Society of GB* v *Boots Cash Chemists (Southern) Ltd* (1952) established that putting medicines which the law required to be sold by a pharmacist on open shelves for customers to pick up themselves did not contravene the strict laws which stated that medicines had to be sold by pharmacists. Placing the medicines on shelves did not amount to an offer but merely an invitation to treat. The offer would come later when the customer took the medicines to the counter and offered to buy them, whereupon a pharmacist would be on hand to accept or not.

Most newspaper adverts will be invitations to treat (particularly if placed by non-business advertisers: *Partridge* v *Crittenden* (1968)) but see the cases of *Carlill* v *Carbolic Smoke Ball Co* (1893) and *Hunter* v *General Accident Fire and Life Insurance Corporation Ltd* (1909) below in which the adverts offered rewards.

Quotations

If A asks B to give A a quotation for goods or services then this is not an offer on A's part to buy those goods or services. The quotation which B gives, on the other hand, may amount to an offer if it is specific enough. A "ballpark" figure or rough guess would not be an offer but a detailed and specific quotation might be, as in the case of *Jaeger Bros Ltd* v *J & A McMorland* (1902) in which the defenders were asked for a very specific price for cargo and responded, "offer 600 tons half one, half three, Govan, Leith, 75s 9d; c.i.f. Hamburg, 80s 9d", which was accepted. They tried to argue that this was a mere quotation and not an offer but the court held that it was specific enough to amount to an offer. The fact that it contained the word "offer" was not of itself enough to make it an offer – the courts will look beyond what the parties think they are doing and look at the character and nature of the activity. However, in this case it did meet the criteria of an offer.

Tender

Businesses are often required to put in a tender for work. This process is common in the construction industry: a number of builders will put forward plans and prices for a job and the party developing the land will choose from these tenders. The tender is the offer and the developer accepts it; the invitation to put the tender in is not an offer.

Willingness to negotiate

Negotiations may precede the actual offer. In the case of *Harvey* v *Facey* (1893), the court had to decide whether a message containing the phrase "Lowest price for Bumper Hall Pen £900" constituted an offer to sell that property or not. This message was sent in response to a request from one party as to whether the other was willing to sell Bumper Hall Pen. Did this reply constitute an offer to sell or not? The court held not; this was a willingness to negotiate and not an offer to sell at that price.

The case of *Philp & Co* v *Knoblauch* (1907) provides another example of the importance of wording in determining intentions. In this case, Knoblauch sent a letter to Philp & Co which stated, "I am offering today Plate Linseed for January/February shipment to Leith and have pleasure in quoting you 100 tons at 41/3, usual Plate terms. I shall be glad to hear if you are buyers and await your esteemed reply." Philp & Co replied by telegraph the following day, accepting this offer by stating, "Accept hundred January/February Plate 41s. 3d, per steamer Leith." The court held that the letter from Knoblauch was definitely an offer and distinguished this case from *Harvey* v *Facey* because it found that a "plain offer" had been made in the usual way of commerce. It was not merely an invitation to start negotiations.

To whom may an offer be made?

An offer can be made to a specific party or to the world at large: in *Carlill* v *Carbolic Smoke Ball Co* (1893) it was held that an offer is valid even if made in an advertisement for a product, as long as the offer itself is clear and demonstrates an intention to be bound. In this case, the manufacturers of a smoke ball declared that they had lodged £1,000 in a bank and that they would pay £100 to anyone who bought their product, used it correctly, but still contracted influenza. This was held to be an effective offer which Mrs Carlill, a member of the public, was able to accept.

Frequently Asked Question

Why is Carlill *not a case of promise?*
If it were decided under the law of promise then the need for offer and acceptance does not arise because the promisor does not need a response from the promisee to be bound by it.

The most straightforward answer is that this is an English case and therefore decided in a legal system that does not recognise promise as a legally enforceable obligation in the same way as Scots law. The court categorised the advertisement as an offer.

However, the Scottish courts did make a decision similar to *Carlill* in the case of *Hunter* v *General Accident Fire and Life Assurance Corporation Ltd* (1909). In this case, Mr Hunter bought a Letts diary which contained a coupon advertising that Letts would pay money to the estate of any customer who registered his name with the head office and who died or was injured in a rail accident within 12 months of so doing. He duly registered his name under the scheme. Unfortunately, Mr Hunter was killed in an accident and his estate claimed the money. Even although a Scottish court could have had the option of deciding this under the law of promise, it decided that the advert in the coupon was an offer just as the newspaper advert was an offer in *Carlill*.

How long does an offer stay open for acceptance? Can it be revoked?

Lapse

An offer will lapse and cease to be capable of acceptance in a number of circumstances.

These are:

(1) *The offer is met by an acceptance* (the contract is then concluded).

(2) *A time limit placed on the offer expires without acceptance having been made* (*Littlejohn* v *Hadwen* (1882)). The offer is no longer available for acceptance.

(3) *No time limit is placed on the offer but a "reasonable period of time" expires without acceptance being made.* What is a reasonable period of time? In the case of *Wylie & Lochhead* v *McElroy & Sons* (1873), the parties were involved in negotiations over iron-work for Wylie & Lochhead's new business premises. The original offer to carry out the work was made in April but that was not accepted until 5 weeks later (and even then, not on identical terms). It was argued by McElroy & Sons that because of the length of the time delay and the fact that iron prices fluctuate on a regular basis the original offer was no longer available for acceptance. The court agreed. The definition of "reasonable period of time" will depend on the type of contract and the conditions around it: in a commercial contract, therefore, the stability of prices and the way that the business is usually done will be taken into account.

(4) *Death, insanity and bankruptcy* all affect offers. If either party dies or the offeror becomes insane or bankrupt then the offer will be deemed or *implied* to have lapsed.

(5) *Counter-offers*: a counter-offer (or qualified acceptance) by the offeree causes the original offer to lapse. See *Wolf & Wolf* v *Forfar Potato Co Ltd* (1984), below. It cannot then be accepted.

(6) *Destruction of subject matter*: the offer will lapse if the subject matter of the offer is destroyed.

(7) *Supervening illegality or impossibility*: if what the offer seeks to do becomes illegal or impossible in law then the offer will lapse.

(8) *Rejection*: if the offer is rejected then it lapses and can no longer be accepted.

Revocation

It is also possible to revoke or take back an offer in certain circumstances. The offeror can revoke the offer during the *locus poenitentiae*. This translates as "the time for repentance" and lasts from the time of the offer until the time of acceptance or for such period as the offeror agrees to keep the offer open or until the offer lapses anyway. The offeror must communicate revocation to the offeree for it to be effective. The rules are as follows:

(1) *Time limit cases – keeping offers open*

If the offeror agrees to keep the offer open for a specified period then he cannot revoke the offer until that time limit expires without being in breach of the promise to keep the offer open (*Littlejohn* v *Hadwen* (1882)).

(2) *Time limit cases – offeree told to accept by deadline*

The wording used may be different from (1) but the effect is the same: revocation before the deadline is a breach of promise.

(3) *Open offers – no time limits*

The offeror can revoke the offer at any time before acceptance. However, revocation may not be necessary because offers not subject to a time limit will still lapse if not accepted within a "reasonable time" (*Wylie & Lochhead* v *McElroy & Sons* (1873)).

(4) *Express revocation within the locus poenitentiae*

Provided that the offeror is not bound by any time limits then he can revoke the offer at any time before acceptance.

ACCEPTANCE

Definition

An acceptance can be verbal or written or implied by actions although the offer may specify what form the acceptance *must* take to be effective. The general rule is that it must be communicated to the offeror; silence does not amount to acceptance (unless both parties actually agree to that). However, the following illustrate some day-to-day situations in which communication takes a form which means that the fact of acceptance need not be known by the offeror for it to take immediate effect.

Acceptance by action

In this case, the acceptance is made by the offeree doing something. A common example is a vending machine. The case of *Thornton* v *Shoe Lane Parking Ltd* (1971) is authority for the point that a vending machine offers its contents (eg chocolate, coffee, parking ticket, etc) and that this offer is accepted by the action of putting money into the machine. The offeror (which would be the owner of the vending machine) does not know that the offer has been accepted at that exact moment but it is nonetheless effective.

Acceptance by action can also be seen in cases of offers made to the general public, as in *Carlill* v *Carbolic Smoke Ball Co* where the acceptance of the offer came about as a result of Mrs Carlill's actions, and there was no notification of her acceptance to the Carbolic Smoke Ball Co. Nevertheless, her actions in buying and using the smoke ball were enough to amount to acceptance because this is what the offer (ie the advert) called for.

Acceptance by post (the postal rule)

Specific rules apply to contracts made by post. The general rule is that an acceptance is effective at the time of posting. This means that the offeror is not aware that the contract is concluded because he does not know when the acceptance has been put in the post.

Lost/delayed post

Difficulties arise when an acceptance is duly posted, but is lost or delayed. The Scottish courts have indicated in the case of *Mason* v *Benhar Coal* (1882) that an acceptance lost in the post did not conclude the contract, which contrasts with the English case of *Household Fire Insurance Co Ltd* v *Grant* (1879), in which it was held that acceptance was valid if it could be proved to be posted, though never delivered. There is no authoritative decision on this in Scots law at the moment, but the English decision seems to be the most logical. All cases are subject to the facts being proved: surely a lost letter is a problem from the point of view of *proving* that it was posted rather than an excuse to deviate from the normal legal rule that acceptance is made as soon as it is posted?

Incorrectly addressed letters of acceptance leading to delayed receipt have been considered in the Scottish case of *Jacobsen, Sons & Co v Underwood & Son Ltd* (1894). A letter of acceptance which missed out part of the offeror's address was delayed and did not reach the offeror within the time limit placed on acceptance. However, it had been posted within that time limit. The court held that posting the letter was enough to satisfy the requirements of the postal rule. In considering the effect of the incorrect address, the court was of the opinion that it did not matter but this was in circumstances where the incorrect address had been used many times by the offeree before and without problems arising. This case suggests that the postal rule should be interpreted strictly but this does not answer the question "what if no address was put on the letter at all – would the postal rule operate to conclude that contract as soon as the letter was placed in the post?" This would probably not be enough to satisfy the rule as the postal service must have some means of fulfilling its role.

Frequently Asked Questions

How can the offeror protect his position?

From an offeror's point of view, the postal rule is unsatisfactory as it leaves him not knowing whether the offer has been accepted (or not) for some time after the event. The usual way to safeguard the offeror's position is to state in any offer that acceptance is considered to be effective, and thus a contract concluded, when the acceptance *arrives* at a particular place (usually an office) or in the hands of a particular person (eg a solicitor or estate agent).

Does the postal rule apply to modern forms of communication?

The postal rule does not apply to telexes or fax machines. These are considered to be methods of instantaneous communication, and will be treated the same way as verbal communications, which means that an acceptance from either of these electronic machines is effective once printed out at the offeror's end. It is likely that the law will treat e-mail as an instantaneous method of communication.

Cancellation or revocation of acceptance

Can acceptance be cancelled, revoked or withdrawn? The general rule is no, whatever method of communication is used, because the contract is concluded as soon as the acceptance is made.

However, the law is clouded in postal cases by the decision in *Dunmore* v *Alexander* (1830) in which the Countess of Dunmore wrote a letter accepting an offer, and on the following day wrote another letter cancelling. Both letters were delivered together. The court held that there was no contract where both were delivered together. This case has been the subject of much controversy; it was distinguished in *Thomson* v *James* (1855) which did not extend this decision to revocation of offers. There it was held that the revocation of an offer had to reach the offeree to be effective. Many academics consider *Dunmore* to be a flawed decision because it does not follow the postal rule to its logical conclusion. It is, of course, an old decision and was made before the postal rule was established in Scots law; but it has not been overruled as yet. In attempting to explain the decision, academic writers say there is no problem if the Countess's first letter is treated as an offer of employment made after preliminary enquiries. The problem of conflict with other authority only arises if the letter is labelled an acceptance (MacQueen and Thomson, para 2.34). If this is how the letter is seen, then it can be considered that *Dunmore* is authority for withdrawal of acceptance – which is flawed.

Qualified acceptance/counter-offer

The general rule is that an acceptance must be unqualified to conclude the contract. If the offeree accepts the offer but subject to certain changes to important aspects of it, then that is called a qualified acceptance (or counter-offer) and does not conclude the contract. It causes the original offer to lapse and there is no contract unless the offeror then accepts that qualified acceptance. This is demonstrated in *Wolf & Wolf* v *Forfar Potato Co* (1984). In this case, an offer was made to sell a certain quantity and type of potatoes. That offer was accepted but subject to certain changes. The court held that those changes meant that the "acceptance" was not really an acceptance at all but a qualified acceptance or counter-offer. The original offer therefore lapsed and the ball was then in the original offeror's court to accept the qualified acceptance or counter-offer or not.

This is quite usual in complex transactions such as transactions in the property market: an offer is made for a house at a particular price with certain material conditions, some but not all of which will be accepted by the offeree. The offeree responds with a qualified acceptance and the offeror accepts or else responds with more qualifications for the offeree to accept.

Qualified acceptance and the Battle of the Forms

It is common for businesses to include their own terms and conditions of trading on their paperwork. However, what happens if one business makes an offer to buy goods using a form which contains all of its own terms and conditions and the offeree business accepts that offer on a form which contains all of *its* terms and conditions which are different? Does this end up in a "non-concludable" battle of offers and counter-offers? If one applies the general rule then the acceptance is a qualified acceptance or counter-offer and so there is no contract.

In resolving this, the courts do apply the general rule but have added a twist. The counter-offer becomes the offer and the conduct of the original offeror in acting as if the contract is concluded becomes the acceptance.

In an exchange of several forms back and forth, the same approach is taken and the last form in becomes the offer: if the other party acts on it, the contract is concluded. This is important to know because it means that the terms and conditions of the contract are contained in *that* form and not in the others: the parties cannot pick and choose the best terms for themselves (*Uniroyal* v *Miller & Co* (1985) and *Continental Tyre & Rubber Co Ltd* v *Trunk Trailer Co Ltd* (1987)).

SUMMARY

To identify whether a contract has been concluded, one must be able to label the different types of activity which make up formation of contract and to use that knowledge to identify the point at which the contract is concluded.

Once an offer is accepted the contract is concluded and the parties are legally bound to carry out their respective obligations under that contract and can enforce their rights gained under it. Neither can cancel the contract because they no longer want to do what has been agreed, except in very limited circumstances. A number of consumer contracts have limited cancellation rights. These include:

(1) certain consumer credit contracts under the Consumer Credit Act 1974 and related statutory instruments;
(2) certain contracts covered by the Consumer Protection (Distance Selling) Regulations 2000; and
(3) certain holiday contracts under the Package Travel, Package Holidays and Package Tours Regulations 1992.

Any other attempt to get out of the contract will have to be done by:

(1) arguing that it is flawed in law; that it is defective, invalid, void, voidable or unenforceable (Chapter 3); or
(2) breaching it and accepting the repercussions of doing that (Chapter 6); or

(3) arguing that it has been terminated through other means (Chapter 7).

Essential Facts

- A contract is formed when an offer is met with an acceptance.
- An offer must be capable of acceptance, it must be communicated in clear, specific terms and it must include the intention to be legally bound. It may be verbal or in writing or in some other form.
- Offers should be distinguished from auctions, invitations to treat, requests for quotations, tenders and willingness to negotiate.
- An offer can be made to a specific party or a class of persons or to the general public.
- An offer does not remain open forever. It will lapse (1) if accepted, (2) on expiry of a time limit set for acceptance, (3) on expiry of a reasonable period of time if it is not to be kept open for a specified period of time, (4) if either party dies or the offeror becomes insane or bankrupt, (5) if it is met with a counter-offer/qualified acceptance, (6) if the subject matter is destroyed before acceptance is made, (7) if what is suggested in the offer becomes illegal or impossible, or (8) if it is rejected.
- An offer can be revoked at any time before acceptance, unless a time period has been set for acceptance, in which case it cannot be revoked during that time period without breaching promise.
- Acceptance can be verbal or written or implied by actions although the offer may specify what form the acceptance *must* take to be effective.
- The general rule is that it must be communicated to the offeror; silence does not amount to acceptance (unless both parties actually agree to that).
- The postal rule applies to contracts made by post. The basic rule is that a contract is concluded as soon as the acceptance is posted.
- Acceptance cannot generally be revoked or cancelled because the acceptance concludes the contract. However, there is controversial case law to suggest that a letter of cancellation posted after a letter of acceptance was effective when both arrived together.
- A counter-offer/qualified acceptance accepts the offer but subject to certain changes. It causes the original offer to lapse so that it is no longer open for acceptance.
- The "battle of the forms" in business causes certain problems for the traditional offer/acceptance model of contract formation.

- The general rule is that, once concluded, a contract cannot be cancelled (unless both parties agree to that). However, some consumer protection legislation does provide cancellation rights for some contracts (eg consumer credit contracts).

Essential Cases

Thornton v Shoe Lane Parking Ltd (1971): example of offer and acceptance by action (slot machine).

Warlow v Harrison (1859): English case suggesting that auctioning goods without a reserve price *does* amount to an offer (but note provisions of s 57(2) of Sale of Goods Act 1979 for those contracts).

Fisher v Bell (1960): flick-knife case – shop window display is invitation to treat.

Pharmaceutical Society of GB v Boots (1952): medicines case – display did not amount to offer; customer offers to buy by taking them to the counter.

Partridge v Crittenden (1968): newspaper advert by *non*-businessman was invitation to treat.

Carlill v Carbolic Smoke Ball Co (1893): the flu and advert case; an advert by a company promising a reward for customers falling ill was an offer.

Hunter v General Accident Fire and Life Insurance Corp Ltd (1909): the diary and the rail passenger case; Scottish authority for advert as offer.

Jaeger Bros Ltd v J & A McMorland (1902): detailed and specific quotation can amount to offer.

Harvey v Facey (1893): Bumper Hall Pen case; offer versus willingness to negotiate.

Philp v Knoblauch (1907): Plate Linseed case; plain offer made in the course of commerce was an offer and not an invitation to treat.

Littlejohn v Hadwen (1882): offer cannot be revoked during period specified for acceptance.

Wylie & Lochhead v McElroy & Sons (1873): iron-work case; offer lapses if not accepted within a reasonable period of time.

Wolf & Wolf v Forfar Potato Co Ltd (1984): counter-offer case; counter-offer causes original offer to lapse.

Mason v Benhar (1882): postal rule – lost in the post. Not a firm decision but indicates that Scots courts would treat acceptance lost in the post as *not* concluding the contract; contrast English case of *Household Fire Insurance Co Ltd v Grant*.

Jacobsen, Sons & Co v Underwood & Son Ltd (1894): postal rule – incorrectly addressed letter still concluded contract.

Dunmore v Alexander (1830): controversial postal rule case involving Countess of Dunmore. Possible to argue that it finds a posted letter of acceptance to have been cancelled when that cancellation arrived at the same time as the acceptance. Illogical.

3 PROBLEMS WITH CONTRACTS

Once a contract has been concluded, both parties are bound to perform their respective obligations under it. However, the fact that a contract has been concluded does not necessarily mean that it is a valid and enforceable contract. It may be flawed in some way and this may affect whether the contract stands or can be challenged. The aim of this chapter is to describe the various problems which may affect a contract and to explain the effect of those problems on the contract and the parties to it. That effect can take a number of forms: a flawed contract may be void, voidable or unenforceable.

VOID

Void means that the contract, although *apparently* formed, is so fundamentally flawed that it is null and has never come into existence. It is worth spending a little time considering this concept. The parties thought that they had a contract; they may even have acted on the strength of it. However, the law finds that it is lacking a vital ingredient and so never existed as a true contract at all; it may be described using various terms: "void", "void *ab initio*", "null". Such an "apparent" contract cannot give any party any rights but, on the other hand, it cannot impose any obligations on them either. Void is not the same as voidable or unenforceable (see below).

If the parties have fulfilled part or all of their obligations under an apparent contract before discovering that it is void, then they cannot use the law of contract to reclaim any money or property passed over under the apparent contract because there is *no* contract. Such claims must be fought under the law of unjustified enrichment. Unjustified enrichment can be used to ensure that there is a "settling up" between parties who acted as if they had a contract but in fact did not in law. Parties may have to seek remedies under unjustified enrichment in the courts if the other parties do not comply voluntarily.

The remedies under unjustified enrichment are:

(1) *Repetition*: money paid over by one of the parties in fulfilling the apparent contract is repaid.

(2) *Restitution*: property transferred by one of the parties in fulfilling the apparent contract is returned.

(3) *Recompense*: a monetary payment is made to cover the loss suffered by one of the parties.

Third parties cannot obtain any rights from a void contract. If A contracts with B to buy B's car but the contract is void (for any number of reasons) then if A sells the car to C, C cannot obtain ownership of it because the original contract (or "apparent contract") is void: ownership never passed to A and one cannot sell what one does not own. The whole chain collapses.

VOIDABLE

A contract which is voidable does exist but only up to the point where it is set aside, either by agreement between the parties or, more likely, by a court on the grounds that it is defective in some way. A contract which is voidable is challengeable on certain legal grounds; it is not so lacking as to be void *ab initio* (ie from the start) but one party may ask the court to set it aside (the words "reduction" or "to reduce a contract" are often used to describe this process). As the contract exists until set aside, it can confer rights on the parties and even on third parties up until that date. Once reduced, it has no effect and this is backdated to its formation.

UNENFORCEABLE

The contract is not necessarily void or voidable but the courts refuse to enforce it for another reason.

THE MAIN PROBLEMS AFFECTING CONTRACTS

The main problems are:

    (i)   lack of consensus
   (ii)   lack of consent
  (iii)   lack of capacity
  (iv)   lack of formality (where required)
   (v)   illegality
  (vi)   restrictions on the freedom to contract
 (vii)   error (misunderstanding and misrepresentation)
(viii)   other prejudicial circumstances.

(i) Lack of consensus

Given that contracts are voluntary obligations, it is essential that both parties have *consensus in idem*; in other words, both are agreeing to the same thing. If they do not agree on the important aspects of the contract then this will prevent the contract from being properly formed at all and it will be void.

The Scottish courts apply an objective test in deciding if the parties have consensus. An objective test is one which does not take into account what the parties themselves think but which applies a benchmark test to decide if consensus has been reached.

Lack of consensus (also known as "dissensus") is illustrated by the case of *Mathieson Gee (Ayrshire) Ltd* v *Quigley* (1952) in which the parties were talking at cross purposes in their offer and acceptance. Mathieson offered to supply plant equipment to clear a pond (ie an offer of hire) whereas Quigley accepted that by confirming his acceptance to an offer to actually clear the pond (ie an acceptance to an offer to do something else). The court held that, notwithstanding what the parties themselves thought, there was no consensus and so no contract.

A lack of consensus may arise out of a mistake or misrepresentation (error), which is dealt with below.

(ii) Lack of consent

It is essential that the parties intend to create a binding legal obligation and so it is necessary to distinguish between social, domestic and gaming arrangements on the one hand and the intention to create binding legal obligations on the other. Some common scenarios in which agreements are made which do not amount to contracts are as follows:

Business arrangements

There is a presumption that agreements made in the course of business do meet the criteria of consent but there may be situations in which negotiations are ongoing and the parties want to come to a non-legally binding agreement on certain issues as part of pre-contractual negotiations. For example, it is common in the purchase and sale of businesses or in commercial leasing for parties to agree "Heads of Agreement" which list key points of the deal (eg price, date of entry, what is to be included in the sale/lease, etc) before moving on to forming a contract. However, the parties have to make it very clear that they do not intend to be legally bound by such an agreement in order to rebut the presumption that these "agreements" are contractual and therefore binding.

This is demonstrated in the case of *Stobo Ltd* v *Morrisons (Gowns) Ltd* (1949) in which the parties made an agreement that the defender would sell on a shop to the pursuer once the defender had bought it. This agreement was made "subject to contract". The defender bought the shop but then refused to sell it on. It was held that there was no contract. The court did not think that the mere use of these words was enough to keep the exchange of letters between the parties in the pre-contractual stage of negotiations but, taken with all the circumstances, no contract had been concluded. See also *Small* v *Fleming* (2003) for a recent example where heads of agreement did not amount to consensus and consent.

If parties have reached this type of pre-contractual agreement and it is breached then the law becomes more complex. A breach of pre-contractual agreements cannot be dealt with by contract law because there is no contract. This problem arose in *Dawson International plc* v *Coats Paton plc* (1988) in which it was held that if one party "breached" this type of pre-contractual agreement then, as a matter of *equity*, the "innocent party" could claim back any money spent honouring the agreement if the one who pulled out had assured the "innocent party" that there *was* a contract (even although there was not).

Family arrangements

The case of *Balfour* v *Balfour* (1919) is an example of the presumption that domestic arrangements do not amount to contracts. In this English case, a husband offered to pay his wife a certain amount of money each month and she accepted. He failed to pay. She sued him for breach of contract but the court held that agreements between spouses did not fulfil the criteria of consent to be legally bound. Of course, this presumption could be rebutted if the money was in settlement of a business debt.

Sponsio ludicra

Gaming arrangements do not create legal obligations either: *Kelly* v *Murphy* (1940) and *Ferguson* v *Littlewoods Pools Ltd* (1997). However, in *Robertson* v *Anderson* (2003) the court enforced a contract in which one person had agreed to share her bingo winnings with another; this was not a gaming arrangement itself but collateral to (ie connected with) the one between the customer and the bingo hall.

(iii) Lack of capacity

Both parties to a contract must have the capacity (legal ability) to enter into that contract. A complete lack of capacity on the part of either party will render the contract void. There are different rules for different legal persons.

Children and young persons

The Age of Legal Capacity (Scotland) Act 1991 applies. The age at which full capacity is reached is now 16.

Children. Children below 16 years of age now have no capacity as a general rule, although there are a number of important exceptions:

(1) A child aged 12 or over may make a will or appoint under a will.

(2) A child of *sufficient understanding* may consent to medical and similar treatment.

(3) Reasonable transactions commonly entered into by children are excluded from the no-capacity rule. This will mean such things as buying sweets and comics in shops, travel in buses and trains. As they get closer to 16, it will apply to contracts relating to after-school work and holiday jobs and the purchase of more expensive items, such as computing or musical equipment.

Young Persons. Young people now acquire full legal capacity to enter into transactions at 16. However, there are further protections for 16 and 17 year-olds. If a person aged 16 or 17 enters into a contract which is a "prejudicial transaction" as defined by the 1991 Act then it may be set aside in certain circumstances. The definition of "prejudicial" has two parts under s 3(2):

(a) the transaction is one which an adult, exercising reasonable prudence, would not have entered into in the circumstances of that young person; and

(b) the transaction has caused or is likely to cause substantial prejudice to the young person.

Frequently Asked Questions

How does a young person get out of a prejudicial transaction?
If the young person wants to get out of that transaction on those grounds then he must apply to the court under s 3 of the Age of Legal Capacity (Scotland) Act 1991 to have it set aside. He has until the day before he reaches his 21st birthday to do this. He cannot do it if the prejudicial transaction is a will (or other testamentary writing), consent to an adoption order, consent to medical, surgical or dental treatment, or relates to his part in civil proceedings. There are three further important restrictions. A young person cannot apply to the court to have a prejudicial transaction set aside if:

(1) the transaction was made in the course of his business trade or profession (s 3(2)(f)); or

(2) he lied about his age and this fraudulent misrepresentation induced the other party into entering into the contract with him (s 3(2)(g)); or

(3) he ratified the contract after the age of 18 despite knowing his right to ask for it to be set aside (s 3(2)(h)).

Only the young person has the right to apply to the court; the other party to the transaction does not.

What circumstances will the court take into account?
The transaction has to be judged by the circumstances at the date entered into.

What is the effect of a successful court action?
The result of a successful application is that the contract is set aside and the parties are returned to their previous positions, subject to the general law relating to voidable transactions.

How can a third party protect his position in contracting with a young person?
Apply to court to have the contract ratified under s 3(3)(j) and the court will decide if it is reasonable or not.

Adults with incapacity

Many adults suffer from mental health or mental disorder problems such as psychiatric problems and dementia. A number of adults are affected by learning difficulties. Under the common law, an "insane" person has no contractual capacity. The Adults with Incapacity (Scotland) Act 2000 provides a legal framework for managing the affairs of incapax adults (primarily for financial and medical matters). It states that an adult (ie someone aged over 16) is incapax if he cannot act or make decisions or communicate decisions or understand decisions or keep a memory of decisions because of a mental disorder. The Act allows for flexibility, however, so that the adult is deemed to have capacity if he can make a decision based on relevant information appropriate to his or her level of understanding and not under any undue pressure.

The 2000 Act reformed the law on who can look after the affairs of an incapax adult. Third parties can now do this under the following measures:

- *Power of Attorney*: this is made by the adult himself while he still has capacity. This may be used by someone diagnosed with dementia who would like to have some control over his future as his condition deteriorates.
- *Guardianship orders*: a third party can apply to court for a continuing order to look after the affairs of the incapax adult.

- *Intervention orders*: a third party can apply to court for an order to allow him to carry out a particular transaction for an incapax adult (eg enter into a contract to sell that person's home to fund residential home costs).

Those appointed as curators and tutors-dative before the Act have continuing authority to act for incapax adults but now do so in their new roles as guardians.

The 2000 Act did not amend s 3(2) of the Sale of Goods Act 1979 which states that "Where necessaries are sold and delivered to a minor or to a person who by reason of mental incapacity or drunkenness is incompetent to contract, he must pay a reasonable price for them." Necessaries are defined in the 1979 Act as goods suitable to the condition in life of the person and to his actual requirements at the time of sale and delivery.

It should be noted that lack of capacity is not the same as *facility and circumvention* which occurs in cases where a vulnerable person is taken advantage of by others and which can have an impact on the validity of the contract (see below).

Intoxicated persons

The level of intoxication through alcohol or drugs or solvent abuse must be very high to result in a loss of capacity (*Taylor* v *Provan* (1864)). The contract will be void but the intoxicated party must challenge the contract as soon as possible after sobering up or lose that protection (*Pollock* v *Burns* (1875)).

Section 3(2) of the Sale of Goods Act 1979 also applies to the purchase of "necessaries" by those who are intoxicated.

Registered companies

A registered company is a legal person in its own right, separate from the shareholders who own it and the directors who run it. A company has full legal capacity and ss 35, 35A and 35B of the Companies Act 1985 (as amended) state that, in dealings with innocent third parties, a company has full capacity regardless of any restrictions contained in its constitution (the Memorandum and Articles of Association). A contract with an innocent third party is therefore *not* rendered void by the fact that the company is acting *ultra vires* (ie outwith its power) but a third party will not have this protection if he knows that the company"s power to agree is restricted by its constitution. Although a company's Memorandum and Articles of Association are registered with the Registrar of Companies, there is no obligation on a third party to investigate their terms before entering into contracts with a company. The capacity of companies will be simplified if and when part 4 of the Company Law Reform Bill is passed because challenges on grounds of lack of capacity will be limited to contracts between the company and its directors or connected persons.

Partnerships

Partnerships (firms) have separate legal personality in Scotland (Partnership Act 1890, s 4(2)), which means that the firm can sue and be sued. Contracts can also be entered into by the partners on behalf of the firm which bind the firm, provided that the partner(s) act within the confines of s 5 of the Partnership Act 1890, which states: "Every partner is an agent of the firm and his other partners for the purpose of the business of the partnership; and the acts of every partner who does any act for carrying on in the usual way business of the kind carried on by the firm of which he is a member bind the firm and his partners, unless the partner so acting has in fact no authority to act for the firm in the particular matter, and the person with whom he is dealing either knows that he has no authority, or does not know or believe him to be a partner."

Partnership law is currently under review but it is likely, following the Joint Report of the Law Commissions (Law Commission No 283 and Scottish Law Commission No 192), that the nature of the separate legal personality will become stronger and apply to all UK partnerships.

Unincorporated bodies

Clubs and associations etc do not have contractual capacity and must contract through their office bearers.

Enemy aliens

Wartime provisions render contracts with enemy aliens void but an accounting between the parties may still be possible after the war whereby any monies paid over in fulfilling the contract can be repaid and property restored (*Cantiere San Rocco* v *Clyde Shipbuilding Co* (1923)).

(iv) Lack of formality

Some contracts *must* be in writing to be valid and these are governed by the Requirements of Writing (Scotland) Act 1995. Section 1 lists those contracts which must be in writing. It states:

(1) Subject to subsection (2) below and any other enactment, writing shall not be required for the constitution of a contract, unilateral obligation or trust.

(2) Subject to subsection (3) below, a written document complying with section 2 of this Act shall be required for–

(a) the constitution of–

(i) a contract or unilateral obligation for the creation, transfer, variation or extinction of a real right in land [except tenancies or rights to occupy land for less than one year under s 1(7), unless these are rolling arrangements];

(ii) a gratuitous unilateral obligation [ie a promise] except an obligation undertaken in the course of business; and

(iii) a trust whereby a person declares himself to be sole trustee of his own property or any property which he may acquire;

(b) the creation, transfer, variation or extinction of a real right in land otherwise than by the operation of a court decree, enactment or rule of law; and

(c) the making of any will, testamentary trust disposition and settlement or codicil.

Frequently Asked Questions

What sort of obligations must be in writing?
Writing is required to form:

- contracts relating to an interest in land (eg buying, selling and leasing houses, farms, factories and other real rights in land)
- promises (except if given in the course of business).

What if a contract which should be in writing is not but the parties act on it anyway?
The Requirements of Writing (Scotland) Act 1995 makes provision to solve this problem under s 1(3) and (4) which replace the old common law rules of *rei interventus* and homologation. Subsections (3) and (4) of the Act state:

"(3) Where a contract, obligation or trust mentioned in subsection (2)(a) above is not constituted in a written document complying with section 2 of this Act, but one of the parties to the contract, a creditor in the obligation or a beneficiary under the trust ('the first person') has acted or refrained from acting in reliance on the contract, obligation or trust with the knowledge and acquiescence of the other party to the contract, the debtor in the obligation or the truster ('the second person')–

(a) the second person shall not be entitled to withdraw from the contract, obligation or trust; and

(b) the contract, obligation or trust shall not be regarded as invalid, on the ground that it is not so constituted, if the condition set out in subsection (4) below is satisfied.

(4) The condition referred to in subsection (3) above is that the position of the first person–

(a) as a result of acting or refraining from acting as mentioned in that subsection has been affected to a material extent; and

(b) as a result of such a withdrawal as is mentioned in that subsection would be adversely affected to a material extent."

These rules also apply to any variation of a contract, obligation or trust.

What does this mean? A contract or unilateral gratuitous obligation (promise) which *should* be in writing under s 2(a) of the Act, but is not, may still be valid and enforceable. This can happen if one of the parties who has a right under the contract (eg a right to receive title to land in exchange for the price) starts doing things or not doing things as if the contract were properly constituted with the other party's knowledge and consent. If he has been affected to a material extent by doing or not doing things as if the contract was written down *and* if he would be materially affected if the other party were to pull out of the contract on the grounds that it was not properly constituted, then the lack of writing is not fatal to that contract and it stands. In applying this section, one must therefore check:

- Is the contract one of those listed in s 1(2) and, therefore, one which should be in writing?
- Has one party with a right under the contract done something (eg started ordering bricks for a new house to be built on the land to be bought under it) or not done something (eg not renewed the lease on his current rented home as he expects to move into the new house soon) in reliance on the contract?
- Does the other party know about that?
- Has the other party acquiesced (this could be a positive act of consent or he could acquiesce by seeing what is going on but not telling the other party to stop)?
- Has the first party been affected to a material extent by what he has done/not done? (Usually, this means – "is he out of pocket?")
- Would he be affected to a material extent if the other party pulled out now?

If the answer to all of these questions is "yes", then the contract is cured under s 1(3) and (4) and is valid and the parties are personally barred from arguing that it is not.

What form of writing is required?
The 1995 Act also sets out rules about the way in which such contracts are to be written.

Formal writing. A contract which requires to be formal must be written and subscribed under s 2 of the 1995 Act (requirements for formality). Thus, where a contract is made up of an offer and an acceptance then it will be signed at the end by the offeror on an offer and by the offeree on the acceptance; a contract set out in one document is subscribed by both parties at the end.

Probative. A contract can be made *probative* (ie self proving in a court action) by attestation (ie by being witnessed) (s 3) or by endorsement with a court certificate (s 4). Only one witness is required and he or she must be 16 or over.

Notarial execution. People who cannot sign contracts because of blind-ness, paralysis or other difficulty can use the device of notarial execution to subscribe contracts under s 9 of the 1995 Act whereby a solicitor, JP or other party listed in the section reads the contract to that person who confirms that they have agreed to its terms and the solicitor or other party then signs on their behalf. The separate matter of probativity is achieved by witnessing or court certificate as before.

Is electronic communication a valid form of writing for the Act?
No. The definition of "writing" still implies that original paper documents are needed. Any moves towards reforming rules on writing have been made in small steps so far. Electronic signatures *are* valid for certain purposes under s 7 of the Electronic Communications Act 2000 but only to prove the authenticity of electronic communication or data. In property law, the Keeper of the Registers of Scotland (who is responsible for holding all title deeds for land in Scotland) allows Automated Registration of Title for Land (although these digital deeds are not a substitute for actual title deeds). However, the general definition of "writing" has not yet been amended to include electronic communication for the creation of formal writing. This does not mean that contracts can never be formed using electronic writing; it only becomes an issue if formal writing is required.

(v) Illegality

The general rule is that illegal contracts (*pacta illicita*) are unenforceable. However, certain contracts which are illegal under *statute* may be void, voidable *or* unenforceable depending on the wording of the statute. A contract can be illegal in whole or in part. There are a number of important points to bear in mind when looking at this aspect of contract law.

General points

(1) Illegal contracts are not *necessarily* immoral or criminal in nature. The definition goes wider than that and can include contracts or clauses within contracts which contravene other provisions such as restrictive covenants in employment contracts.

(2) There is a difference between contracts concluded for an illegal purpose and contracts which are performed illegally:

- If the contract is formed for an illegal purpose then it is unenforceable. This can arise in two situations. First, the illegal purpose may be clear from the contract itself. This was demonstrated in the case of *Barr* v *Crawford* (1983), in which the contract was for a bribe to be paid by a pub landlady to members of the licensing board. That was a *prima facie* (on the face of it) illegal contract. Secondly, the contract may be for a legitimate purpose on the face of it but the parties know that it is really for an illegal purpose. This is shown in the case of *Pearce* v *Brooks* (1866) in which a contract for the hire of a coach to a prostitute to allow her to ply her trade was held to be illegal.

- Alternatively, the contract may be concluded for a legitimate purpose but one or both of the parties may perform it in a way which breaches a particular law. This occurred in the case of *Dowling & Rutter* v *Abacus Frozen Foods Ltd (No 2)* (2002), in which two parties had a contract whereby one, the employment agency Dowling & Rutter, supplied labour to the other, Abacus. That is not an illegal contract in itself. However, Dowling & Rutter supplied illegal immigrants to do the work. The way in which this contract was performed therefore breached immigration legislation. However, Dowling & Rutter did not know that the workers were illegal immigrants and the court held that it was entitled to be flexible in the way in which it decided how this form of illegality would affect the contract and the parties. It decided that an equitable remedy would be to allow the party which had performed the contract illegally – Dowling & Rutter – to recover its fees for the supply of labour. This case would probably have been decided differently had Dowling & Rutter known about its breach of legislation. The important point to note is that illegal performance of a contract does not *automatically* render it unenforceable.

(3) Contracts or parts of contracts may be illegal by statute or by common law. In the former case, the wording of the statute will describe what it is about the contract or clause which fails to meet this criteria and will state the effect of that particular illegality on the contract (ie whether it is void or simply unenforceable). Common law illegality is defined through its case law and the cases must be analysed to identify the problem and the effect (see below).

(4) Even if the parties to such a contract have full capacity and have reached consensus on the contract, they cannot "opt out" of these rules.

Common law illegality

Common law does not allow contracts which are contrary to public policy to be enforced. The following categories have all been established as being illegal at common law.

(1) Criminal contracts: a contract to steal a car to order would be illegal and unenforceable.

(2) Contracts which promote sexual immorality: given that public policy reflects social mores of the day, this category is likely to cover different things at different times, although, of course, if the activity contemplated by the contract is actually illegal then it will fall foul under "criminal contracts".

(3) Contracts which interfere with the court system (such as bribing witnesses) or which try to bar one party from seeking legitimate redress through the courts are illegal.

(4) An important category of contracts (or more likely clauses within contracts) which are illegal at common law are contracts in restraint of trade, also known as restrictive covenants. They are found in three main areas:

- employment contracts;
- sale and purchase of businesses; and
- solus agreements.

Employment contracts. These clauses are put into contracts of employment by employers to try to prevent the employee from working within a certain geographical area or with a competitor of the employer for a designated period of time after the employee leaves the service of the employer. The presumption is that these clauses are unenforceable *unless* the restriction meets three criteria:

- it must protect legitimate business interests of the employer (*Deacons (a firm)* v *Bridge* (1984));
- it must be reasonable (the onus being on the employer to show reasonableness);
- it must be in the public interest.

If an employee does breach the restrictions placed on him in the contract then the employer can go to court and ask for a court order known as an interdict, which will prohibit the employee from continuing to work for the rival business.

The court will take the following matters into account when deciding whether to enforce the restrictive covenant and issue an interdict:

(i) Legitimate business interests. In *Bluebell Apparel Ltd* v *Dickinson* (1978), Bluebell manufactured Wrangler jeans. Dickinson, the employee, knew Bluebell's trade secrets and was a manager with the company. The court upheld a restrictive covenant which prohibited him from disclosing the trade secrets to any unauthorised person and from working for any competitor for 2 years after leaving Bluebell's employment. He left the company and went to work for Levi, a competitor. Bluebell was entitled to protect trade secrets which Dickinson had been privy to during his course of employment with the company. The court will consider the position held by the employee (eg the more senior the employee and the greater access he has to confidential information, the more likely the court will be to enforce the restrictive covenant).

(ii) Restrictions in geographical area and time limits. The court will look at the location of the business and consider whether the geographical limit is reasonable. A business located in a sparsely populated rural area is more likely to get away with stating a larger radius within which the employee should not work than one located in a busy city centre. The following cases demonstrate this point:

- *Stewart* v *Stewart* (1899) – a work ban as a photographer within a 20-mile exclusion zone around Elgin was reasonable;
- *Dallas McMillan & Sinclair* v *Simpson* (1989) – a restriction prohibiting a former partner in a firm from working for 3 years within a 20-mile radius of Glasgow Cross was not reasonable even although the clause

actually stated that it was agreed by all of the parties that both the time limit and the geographical limit were reasonable.

The court will look at the type of business and decide if it merits a long ban on working for a rival or not. Fast-moving industries prone to technological change and fast-moving markets are unlikely to get away with longer time bans.

(iii) Severability. If a contract contains some restrictions which are reasonable and some which are not, is the entire restrictive covenant unenforceable? It will depend on whether the different elements are severable, ie capable of being separated out from the others and applied separately. This issue concerns the drafting of clauses. In *Mulvein* v *Murray* (1908) it was held that the court will not delete unenforceable parts, leaving any reasonable parts which can stand alone. This has led to the standard practice, when drafting restrictive covenants with different elements in them, of using separate clauses for each restriction rather than lumping them together in one clause.

Sale and purchase of business. The purchaser will not want the seller to set up a new rival business nearby. The purchaser of a business will try to protect the goodwill of the business and will include a restrictive covenant in the contract for the purchase and sale of the business: in this context such a clause is more commonly called a restraint of trade clause. In deciding enforceability the same criteria apply as for employer–employee contracts; but the courts are more likely to enforce such business-to-business contracts because of the greater equality in bargaining position and the fact that legitimate business interest in enforcing the clause will be easier to prove.

The following two cases illustrate how the courts have treated these clauses:

- *Nordenfelt* v *Maxim Nordenfelt Guns and Ammunition Co Ltd* (1894) – a worldwide ban on operating in international arms dealing for 25 years was reasonable because of the specialised nature of the business and the fact that purchasers of guns and ammunition were sovereign states and therefore limited in number;
- *Dumbarton Steamboat Co Ltd* v *Macfarlane* (1899) – a 10-year UK-wide ban on operating a carriers business was not reasonable because the business which had been sold had only operated on the West coast of Scotland and not throughout the UK. There were therefore no UK-wide interests to protect.

Solus agreements. Solus agreements are made between a wholesaler/distributor and a retailer who agrees to stock only that wholesaler/distributor's brand (usually in return for discounts). This type of agreement is called a solus agreement and may or may not be included in another contract between the parties (the most common being if the wholesaler leases the business premises to the retailer too). These agreements can be enforced if reasonable. In the case of *Esso Petroleum Co Ltd* v *Harpers Garages (Stourport) Ltd* (1968) a 21-year solus agreement was held to be unenforceable. The Competition Act 1998 also prohibits price fixing and cartels.

Illegality under statute

An Act of Parliament or an Act of the Scottish Parliament may prohibit certain contracts from being made (express illegality) or it may prohibit certain activities, which may render a contract to do such a thing illegal and void or not enforceable (implied illegality). The wording of the statute needs to be looked at carefully to establish the effect that contravening the Act will have on the contract. Performance of the contract may breach the provisions of a statute or an item of secondary legislation; the case of *Dowling & Rutter* v *Abacus Frozen Foods Ltd (No 2)* (above) seems to suggest that the court will be flexible in interpreting the effect of this on the contract and the parties.

(vi) Restrictions on the freedom to contract

In addition to the problems of illegality discussed above, there are other restrictions on the ability of parties to contract freely and these restrictions may affect their contract (or certain parts of it) and prevent it from being enforced.

There is a wide and growing range of consumer protection laws and related measures (much of which come from the European Union), which has a serious impact on what can and cannot be agreed between parties. This is often the case when one of the parties is a consumer although not all restrictions are limited to protecting consumers. These measures restrict the ability of the parties to contract freely. It should be noted at the outset that there is no single definition of consumer and so the relevant definition will be given under each measure. The key principles and provisions to be examined here are:

- Common law and exclusion clauses
- Unfair Contract Terms Act 1977
- Sale of Goods Act 1979

- Unfair Terms in Consumer Contracts Regulations 1999
- Consumer Credit Act 1974
- Carriage of Goods By Sea Act 1992

Common law and exclusion clauses

Any attempt to exclude an obligation or limit liability for breach of contract or for negligence or any other obligation will be looked at very carefully by the courts. Such a clause will be applied *contra proferens*, ie against the party trying to rely on that clause to escape paying out for those breaches, if it is at all ambiguous (*W & S Pollock* v *Macrae* (1922) and *Smith* v *UMB Chrysler and South Wales Switchgear Ltd* (1978)).

Although the enforceability of exclusion and limitation clauses is still a matter for the common law, many of these clauses are now subject to the statutory controls of the Unfair Contract Terms Act 1977 and the Unfair Terms in Consumer Contracts Regulations 1999.

Unfair Contract Terms Act 1977 ("UCTA")

Parts II and III of UCTA apply to Scotland. The purpose of this Act insofar as it applies to Scotland is "to impose further limits on the extent to which … civil liability can be avoided by means of contract terms".

Civil liability may arise in cases of delict or contract. If one party breaches his duty in delict or contract then that party would usually be liable to compensate the other party for that breach (the exact remedy would depend on the type of breach – see Chapter 6 for remedies for breach of contract). A party might try to limit or exclude his liability in advance of any breach by including a limitation clause or an exclusion clause in the contract itself. Nevertheless, even if the other party agrees to that limitation clause or that exclusion clause, UCTA may operate to render these types of clause void or unenforceable.

However, UCTA does not apply to all contracts, nor to all exclusion clauses and the provisions must be checked carefully when applying it. UCTA applies as follows.

(a) Attempts to avoid liability for death or personal injury. Section 16(1)(a) of UCTA covers attempts to limit or exclude liability for death or personal injury arising out of a breach of *duty*.

What contracts does s 16 apply to? Section 15 lists the contracts to which ss 16–18 apply. These include a contract (or the relevant part of a contract) which:

"(a) relates to the transfer of the ownership or possession of goods from one person to another (with or without work having been done on them);

(b) constitutes a contract of service or apprenticeship;

(c) relates to services of whatever kind, including (without prejudice to the foregoing generality) carriage [although this is subject to subs (3)(b)], deposit and pledge, care and custody, mandate, agency, loan and services relating to the use of land;

(d) relates to the liability of an occupier of land to persons entering upon or using that land;

(e) relates to the grant of any right or permission to enter upon or use land not amounting to an estate or interest in the land."

The definition of affected contracts is therefore wide and includes:

- contracts for buying and selling goods and services
- employment contracts
- contracts which allow one party to use land without creating an interest in it (eg a field being used by the local school for a fete)
- contracts of carriage: although contracts of carriage are included in this list, there are specific rules where carriage is by ship or hovercraft under s 15(3)(b) which states that both parties must be dealing in the course of business, or one party is and one party is not (ie the party who is not is deemed a "consumer"). That rule also affects contracts of marine salvage and towage and of charterparty of ships or hovercraft.

UCTA does *not* apply to:

- insurance contracts (s 15(3)(a)(i)), or
- certain business formation and dissolution processes such as company or partnership formation or dissolution (s 15(3)(a)(i)).

Non-contractual notices. Section 16 also applies to non-contractual notices (s 16(1)): these are notices which have not been properly incorporated in the contract but which are nevertheless covered by UCTA (see Chapter 4 on how contractual terms are incorporated into contracts).

What does UCTA, s 16 prohibit? No one can exclude or limit liability if the breach of *duty* leads to death or personal injury. However, the breach of duty must arise in the course of business or occupation of premises used for business. Section 16(1) of UCTA states that "where a term of a contract or a provision of a notice given to persons generally or to particular persons

purports to exclude or restrict liability for breach of duty arising in the
course of any business, or from occupation of any premises used for business
purposes of the occupier, that term or provision:

(a) shall be **void** in any case where such exclusion or restriction is in
respect of death or personal injury" (emphasis added).

What is breach of duty? Section 16 states that the liability must arise
from a breach of duty. "Breach of duty" is defined in s 25 as a breach:

"(a) of any obligation, arising from the express or implied terms of a
contract, to take reasonable care or exercise reasonable skill in the
performance of the contract;

(b) of any common law duty to take reasonable care or exercise
reasonable skill [but not any stricter duty];

(c) of the duty of reasonable care imposed by section 2(1) of the
Occupiers' Liability (Scotland) Act 1960."

It will therefore include negligence claims.

When does this apply? The breach must occur in the course of business
or as a result of use of business premises. It is not necessary that the party or
parties to whom it is addressed (ie those who would be killed or injured) be
a consumer.

What is the effect of s 16(1)(a)? This is a total prohibition – it cannot
be done. Section 16(3) makes it clear that even if the other party agrees to
or is aware of that restriction in the contract or notice then that *of itself* is
not enough to indicate that he "knowingly and voluntarily" accepted the
risk (which is particularly important in delict cases where there is a defence
of consent for which such a contract might be useful evidence). Thus, for
example, if a person paid money and signed a contract to take part in a
bungee jump and was injured because the rope was not properly secured,
he might be told that the bungee operator was not liable to compensate
him for that injury because the contract had a clause in it denying all
liability. Provided the bungee operator is operating as a business then s 16
would apply and liability would not be avoided: the injured party could sue,
notwithstanding the fact that he had appeared to agree otherwise.

Summary. In order to apply UCTA to a contract or clause in a contract
which purports to limit civil liability for death or personal injury arising out
of breach of duty (usually negligence) in Scotland, check the following:

- Is the contract listed under s 15 of UCTA?
- Is there a contractual term or non-contractual notice which attempts to exclude, restrict or limit liability for death or personal injury?
- Is the party who is trying to avoid liability operating in the course of a business (or using business premises) under s 16?
- Does the clause cover a breach of duty as defined in s 25?

If the answer to all of these questions is yes then the exclusion clause is void.

(b) Other attempts to limit/exclude liability for breach of duty.
Section 16 also operates to limit (although not totally prohibit) other attempts at excluding or limiting liability for breach of duty which might result in loss other than death or personal injury. In these cases, subs (1)(b) applies so that any other attempt in a contract or notice to exclude or limit liability "shall ... have no effect if it was not fair and reasonable to incorporate the term in the contract [or to put it in the notice]".

Thus, for example, if a plumber entered into a contract with a home-owner to install a new shower and the contract stated "No liability is accepted for any flooding caused by any works carried out in fulfilment of this contract" and the bathroom was flooded due to the plumber's negligence or failure to exercise due care and skill, then s 16(1)(b) would have to be applied to that clause to ascertain if it was allowed to stand or whether it was rendered useless by UCTA.

What is fair and reasonable? Section 24 sets out the general reasonableness test and, for the purposes of s 16, in the case of a contractual term, it states that "regard shall be had only to the circumstances which were, or ought reasonably to have been, known to or in the contemplation of the parties to the contract at the time the contract was made" and, in respect of a non-contractual notice, "regard shall be had to all the circumstances obtaining when the liability arose".

Limitation clauses. Section 24(3) also sets out a reasonableness test for clauses which do not exclude liability but which try to limit liability by capping it at a certain level. Thus, for example, the plumber's contract might have said, "In the event of any flooding being caused by works undertaken by me, then liability will be limited to £500 maximum." Although better than nothing, this clause would still leave the householder out of pocket if damage ran to thousands rather than hundreds of pounds.

In this type of contract/notice, the reasonableness test allows the following to be taken into consideration in determining if that amount is "fair and reasonable": "(a) the resources which the party seeking to rely on that term could expect to be available to him for the purpose of meeting the liability should it arise; (b) how far it was open to that party to cover himself by insurance." This is therefore a subjective test because it takes into account the personal circumstances of the party seeking to rely on that limitation.

Section 24(4) places the onus of proving that the term/provision is fair and reasonable on the party trying to rely on the exclusion or limitation.

Summary. In order to apply UCTA to a contract or clause in a contract which purports to exclude or limit civil liability for *other* losses arising out of breach of duty (usually negligence) in Scotland, check the following:

- Is the contract listed under s 15 of UCTA?
- Is there a contractual term or non-contractual notice which attempts to exclude or limit liability for loss (other than death or personal injury)?
- Is the party who is trying to exclude or limit liability operating in the course of a business under s 16?
- Does the clause cover a breach of duty as defined in s 25?
- If it is an exclusion clause, is it fair and reasonable under s 24? If it is a limitation clause, is it fair and reasonable under s 24(3)?

If the answer to the final question is no then the exclusion or limitation clause has no effect.

(c) Breach of consumer or standard form contracts. Section 17 deals with the type of exclusion or limitation clause which attempts to exclude or limit liability for breach of *contract* (rather than the other breaches of duty covered by s 16).

Breach of contract is dealt with in Chapter 6. Generally, if one party fails to perform his part of the contract or performs it badly then he is in breach of that contract and certain remedies can be taken against him, which can include having to pay damages to the non-breaching party. However, one party may try to exclude or limit liability for breach of contract by stipulating in the contract that an obligation which would otherwise be imposed on him is excluded or that liability for breach or non-performance is limited in some way. In the case of consumer contracts or standard form contracts, s 17 states that such exclusions or limitations must be fair and reasonable.

What is a consumer contract? Section 25 defines this as: "a contract in which – (a) one party to the contract deals, and the other party to the contract ('the consumer') does not deal or hold himself out as dealing, in the course of a business, and (b) in the case of a contract such as is mentioned in s 15(2)(a) of this Act [ie of sale of goods or supply of goods], the goods are of a type ordinarily supplied for private use or consumption".

What is a standard form contract? This is not defined in UCTA. Not all contracts are individually negotiated with each party negotiating and agreeing the individual terms in any detail. The price and payment details might be filled in and the contract signed by both parties but very often the rest of the contract is pre-printed. A standard form contract is one such pre-printed contract. The case of *McCrone* v *Boots Farm Sales Ltd* (1981) found that conditions of sale could be covered as a standard form contract under s 17.

Summary. In order to apply UCTA to a contract or clause in a contract which purports to exclude or limit civil liability for breach of *contract* in Scotland, check the following:

- Is the contract listed under s 15 of UCTA?
- Is it a consumer contract under s 25 or is it a standard form contract?
- Is there a contractual term which attempts to exclude or limit liability for breach of contract?
- Is the clause fair and reasonable under s 17?

If the answer to the final question is no then the clause will have no effect.

(d) Indemnities in consumer contracts. An indemnity is where one party, A, is entitled to claw back monies paid out by A from another party, B. An indemnity clause which makes a consumer liable to indemnify the other party for any liability which that party incurs as a result of breach of duty or contract can be imposed on a consumer only if it is fair and reasonable to do so (s 18). The liability to be covered by the indemnity must arise in the course of business (or from occupation of premises used for business purposes).

Taking the example of the plumber's contract mentioned above, an indemnity clause in it might state that the consumer had to indemnify the plumber for all loss arising out of the plumber's breach of duty or contract, including any monies which the plumber had to pay out to neighbours for flood damage if he accidentally cut through the mains water pipe for the whole town: this would not be fair and reasonable under s 18.

Summary. An indemnity clause can be included in a consumer contract only if it is fair and reasonable (s 18).

(e) Sale of goods and supply of goods. UCTA also has implications for contracts for the sale of goods and for the supply of goods, which will be dealt with below.

Sale of Goods Act 1979

The Sale of Goods Act 1979 implies certain terms into contracts for the sale of goods and UCTA specifies when these implied terms can be excluded and when they cannot. Most of the provisions of the Sale of Goods Act 1979 apply to all contracts of sale, regardless of whether the contract is a consumer contract or not.

What is a contract of sale? Section 2(1) defines a contract of sale as "a contract by which the seller transfers or agrees to transfer the property in goods to the buyer for a money consideration, called the price". This does not include barter or exchange. Note that there is no distinction between a buyer who is a consumer and one who buys in the course of business, which means that, unless a section specifically refers to this distinction, the same definition applies to all buyers.

There are a number of implied terms:

Section 10: Stipulations as to time. The general presumption is that time is not of the essence in respect of the time of payment. This means that late payment is not automatically a material breach of this type of contract. However, the presumption can be rebutted by the terms of the contract.

Section 12: Title. There is an implied term that the seller has the right to sell the goods in question and that they are not burdened with any charge etc and that the buyer will be able to enjoy them freely. The exception is found in subs (3) which states that the contract or circumstances may show that the seller is only in a position to transfer "such title as he or a third person may have".

Frequently Asked Question

Can this be excluded in the contract?

Section 20(2) of UCTA states that this implied term cannot be excluded in *any* contract. Any contractual term which purports to do that will be void. This applies whether the contract is a consumer contract, as defined in UCTA, or a business-to-business contract.

Section 13: Description. There is an implied term that a good sold by description will correspond with that description.

Frequently Asked Question

Can this be excluded in the contract?

Section 20(2) of UCTA prohibits the exclusion of this implied term in consumer contracts but allows exclusion in other cases if "fair and reasonable". Guidance on what is "fair and reasonable" is given in Schedule 2 to the Act.

Section 14: Quality and fitness. If a seller sells *in the course of business*, then certain terms are implied by the Sale of Goods Act 1979 into the contract. This section will not apply if the seller is not selling in the course of business and so will not apply to private sales such as car boot sales – unless, of course, the seller is running that activity as a business. These terms are implied, which means that although the parties may not express these terms in their contract, which can be written or verbal, the law will do it for them.

The goods must be of satisfactory quality and this standard is set out in s 2A of the 1979 Act, which states: "For the purposes of this Act, goods are of satisfactory quality if they meet the standard that a reasonable person would regard as satisfactory, taking account of any description of the goods, the price (if relevant) and all the other relevant circumstances." Section 2B expands on this definition by setting out further criteria to check this against.

Frequently Asked Question

Can this be excluded in the contract?

Again, s 20(2) of UCTA does not allow these implied terms to be excluded in consumer contracts at all and allows exclusion in other contracts only if it is "fair and reasonable" to do so.

Section 15: Samples. Some goods are sold by sample, meaning that the buyer will order goods on the basis of seeing a sample. For example, a fabric warehouse business might order 30 bolts of fabric on the basis of a small sample and, under this section, it has a right to expect the bulk to correspond with the sample and to be free from any defect, making their quality unsatisfactory, which would not have been apparent on reasonable examination of the sample.

Frequently Asked Question

Can this be excluded in the contract?
Section 20(2) of UCTA does not allow this implied term to be excluded in consumer contracts but does allow exclusion in other contracts if it is fair and reasonable.

Similar restrictions apply to attempts to exclude implied terms under the Supply of Goods (Implied Terms) Act 1973.

Unfair Terms in Consumer Contracts Regulations 1999 (SI 1999/2083)

Many pieces of secondary legislation are made to add detail to the primary Act of Parliament or Act of the Scottish Parliament. However, much secondary legislation is now made in order to implement European Community laws; and these Regulations fall into the latter category. The Unfair Terms in Consumer Contracts Regulations 1999 (the Regulations) implemented the European Directive EC/93/3 on Unfair Terms in Consumer Contracts. This should be borne in mind because the scope and definitions found in the Regulations differ from those of UCTA. It will often be necessary to apply both UCTA and the Regulations to a particular contract or one may apply when the other does not. UCTA applies to consumer and business-to-business contracts (although different measures affect them in different ways) but the Regulations apply only to consumer contracts.

Scope of the Regulations. Regulation 4 states that "[t]hese Regulations apply in relation to unfair terms in contracts concluded between a seller or supplier and a consumer". The regulations apply if: (i) the seller or supplier is dealing in the course of business (it can be a natural or a legal person: ie individuals, companies, firms and other business organisations are all covered by this definition) *and* (ii) the consumer is a "natural person" acting for purposes outwith his usual trade or profession (therefore companies and firms would not be included in that definition, even if dealing outwith their usual business).

How do the Regulations affect contracts?

Regulation 5 sets out the basic focus of the Regulations: "A contractual term which has not been individually negotiated shall be regarded as unfair if, contrary to the requirement of good faith, it causes significant imbalance in the parties' rights and obligations arising under the contract, to the detriment of the consumer." If a contractual term is deemed to be unfair by the Regulations then it is not binding on the consumer under Regulation 8 but the rest of the contract will stand if it can continue in existence without that offending term.

The key issues are considered here.

When is a contractual term not individually negotiated?

Many contracts are in standard form as discussed above. Regulation 5(2) presumes that a contractual term has not been individually drafted, and therefore falls under the scope of the Regulations, "where it has been drafted in advance and the consumer has therefore not been able to influence the substance of the term". Regulation 5(3) recognises that some parts of the contract may be individually negotiated while other parts are not and applies the Regulations to those terms which have not been individually negotiated, thus avoiding parties being able to escape the effect of the Regulations by mixing up contracts with some pre-printed terms and some apparently individually negotiated ones. The onus on showing that a term has been individually negotiated lies with the seller or supplier.

What is an unfair term?

Schedule 2 to the Regulations has an "indicative and non-exhaustive list of terms which may be regarded as unfair". These are:

"Terms which have the object or effect of –

(a) excluding or limiting the legal liability of a seller or supplier in the event of the death of a consumer or personal injury to the latter resulting from an act or omission of that seller or supplier;

(b) inappropriately excluding or limiting the legal rights of the consumer vis-à-vis the seller or supplier or another party in the event of total or partial non-performance or inadequate performance by the seller or supplier of any of the contractual obligations, including the option of offsetting a debt owed to the seller or supplier against any claim which the consumer may have against him;

(c) making an agreement binding on the consumer whereas provision of services by the seller or supplier is subject to a condition whose realisation depends on his own will alone;

(d) permitting the seller or supplier to retain sums paid by the consumer where the latter decides not to conclude or perform the contract, without providing for the consumer to receive compensation of an equivalent amount from the seller or supplier where the latter is the party cancelling the contract;

(e) requiring any consumer who fails to fulfil his obligation to pay a disproportionately high sum in compensation;

(f) authorising the seller or supplier to dissolve the contract on a discretionary basis where the same facility is not granted to the consumer, or permitting the seller or supplier to retain the sums paid for services not yet supplied by him where it is the seller or supplier himself who dissolves the contract;

(g) enabling the seller or supplier to terminate a contract of indeterminate duration without reasonable notice except where there are serious grounds for doing so;

(h) automatically extending a contract of fixed duration where the consumer does not indicate otherwise, when the deadline fixed for the consumer to express his desire not to extend the contract is unreasonably early;

(i) irrevocably binding the consumer to terms with which he had no real opportunity of becoming acquainted before the conclusion of the contract;

(j) enabling the seller or supplier to alter the terms of the contract unilaterally without a valid reason which is specified in the contract;

(k) enabling the seller or supplier to alter unilaterally without a valid reason any characteristics of the product or service to be provided;

(l) providing for the price of goods to be determined at the time of delivery or allowing a seller of goods or supplier of services to increase their price without in both cases giving the consumer the corresponding right to cancel the contract if the final price is too high in relation to the price agreed when the contract was concluded;

(m) giving the seller or supplier the right to determine whether the goods or services supplied are in conformity with the contract, or giving him the exclusive right to interpret any term of the contract;

(n) limiting the seller's or supplier's obligation to respect commitments undertaken by his agents or making his commitments subject to compliance with a particular formality;

(o) obliging the consumer to fulfil all his obligations where the seller or supplier does not perform his;

(p) giving the seller or supplier the possibility of transferring his rights and obligations under the contract, where this may serve to reduce the guarantees for the consumer, without the latter's agreement;

(q) excluding or hindering the consumer's right to take legal action or exercise any other legal remedy, particularly by requiring the consumer to take disputes exclusively to arbitration not covered by legal provisions, unduly restricting the evidence available to him or imposing on him a burden of proof which, according to the applicable law, should lie with another party to the contract."

Effect of term. If a term is unfair because it causes a significant imbalance in the rights and obligations of each party, with the consumer coming off worse, then it does not bind the consumer. The court will consider each term on its merits (*Director General of Fair Trading* v *First National Bank* (2002)).

Who polices the Regulations? Under the Enterprise Act 2002, the Office of Fair Trading (OFT) now has responsibility to deal with complaints that a term is unfair under the Regulations and the OFT can consider complaints and raise court proceedings to obtain an interdict to prevent the offending term from being used by the party seeking to rely on it (under Regulations 10 and 11). Prior to the Enterprise Act, this action was taken by the Director General of Fair Trading. Certain qualifying bodies also have these rights. The qualifying bodies are listed under Schedule 1 to the Regulations and are as follows:

- The Information Commissioner
- The Gas and Electricity Markets Authority
- The Director General of Electricity Supply for Northern Ireland
- The Director General of Telecommunications
- The Director General of Water Services
- The Rail Regulator
- Every weights and measures authority in GB
- The Department of Enterprise, Trade and Investment in Northern Ireland
- The Financial Services Authority.

Consumer Credit Act 1974

A detailed discussion of consumer credit protection is not appropriate here but any student of contract should be aware that the Consumer Credit Act 1974 (as amended) and the many pieces of secondary legislation made under that Act apply in these cases and regulate the formation and content of consumer credit contracts, from loans to overdrafts to credit and store cards.

Carriage of Goods By Road Act 1965 and Carriage of Goods By Sea Acts 1971 and 1992

The contract of carriage has a long history and is subject to its own specific body of law, much of which has developed out of international agreements. The Carriage of Goods By Road Act 1965 implements the Convention on the Contract for the International Carriage of Goods by Road and the Carriage of Goods By Sea Act 1971 implements the Hague Rules as amended by the Brussels Protocol 1968 (the Hague-Visby Rules). Any contract of carriage must therefore be considered in the context of the applicable rules.

(vii) Error (misunderstanding and misrepresentation)

The validity of a contract can also be affected if either or both parties to it enter into the contract under a misunderstanding about some aspect of the contract or matters relating to it. This is called the law of error. Error can take a number of forms and its *effect* on the contract will vary according to the circumstances. Error may render a contract void, voidable or unenforceable. Alternatively, it may have no effect at all.

The law of error is difficult. The Scottish Law Commission recognises that "it is impossible to harmonise in a convincing manner the institutional and judicial pronouncements on error" (SLC, *Constitution and Proof of Voluntary Obligations: Abortive Constitution*, Memo No 37). However, there are two very general rules which can be used as a starting point:

- Error can lead to a lack of consensus in limited circumstances.
- Uninduced unilateral error (ie a mistake made by one of the parties without any inducement by anything the other party has said or done) will not usually affect the contract.

These are very loose rules and the effect of error has to be considered in each individual case. The law student can begin to make sense of the subject by asking three questions, which will identify the type of error, and then noting the effect of that type of error on the contract. The three questions to consider are:

(1) Who made the error?
(2) What caused the error to be made?
(3) Is it an essential error or not?

(1) Who made the error?

The error may be unilateral or bilateral.

Unilateral error. The error is made by only one of the parties to the contract.

Effect on the contract. The general rule for *written* onerous contracts is that the contract is valid and enforceable, notwithstanding that one party has made a mistake about the nature of the obligation he is undertaking in the contract, even if the error is essential (see below at Question (3) for a discussion of what is meant by "essential"). Authority for this is provided by *Stewart* v *Kennedy* (1890). This was the position in *Spook Erection (Northern) LW* v *Kaye* (1990), in which the sellers of a property made an uninduced unilateral error about the length of the lease affecting the property. They thought that it ran for 990 years, when in fact it was a 99-year lease. They argued that this made the contract void but the court disagreed and upheld the contract.

The exception to this general rule is if the mistake was induced by the other party (see below at Question (2)).

What about other contracts? In other contracts (ie those which are not written onerous contracts), the general rule is that a unilateral error will not affect the contract. The exceptions to the general rule are:

- the error was induced by the other party (see below at Question (2)); or
- the contract is a gratuitous contract (*Hunter* v *Bradford Property Trust* (1970)); or
- the error is so basic as to lead to a lack of *consensus in idem* because the contract is void anyway; or
- *possibly*, if the other party realises that the mistake has been made and tries to take advantage of it (this is the position supported by *Steuart's Trustees* v *Hart* (1875) which has been disputed in later cases but most recently quoted with approval in *Angus* v *Bryden* (1992)).

Bilateral error. There is error on both sides. The question which then has to be asked is: have they both made the same error (common error) or have they made different errors and formed different opinions about what has been agreed (mutual error)?

Effect of common error. If the mistake is an essential error then the contract is void (*Hamilton* v *Western Bank* (1861)).

Effect of mutual error. If the error is essential then the contract is void because of lack of *consensus in idem*. If the error is incidental then the contract is valid and enforceable, unless the error is induced by misrepresentation (see below at Question (2)).

(2) What caused the error?

How did the mistake or error occur in the first place: was it uninduced (ie not caused by anything the other party said or did) or was it induced (ie caused by the actions or words of the other party)? The contract is much more likely to be void or voidable if the error is induced.

Uninduced error (ie error not caused by anything the other party said or did). There are two types of uninduced error:

    (i) error of expression; and
    (ii) error of intention.

(i) Error of expression. This can arise in two scenarios. First, one or both of the parties may express the terms of the contract incorrectly by mistake. This will usually be a clerical error such as misspelling a word so that it has a different meaning from the one intended or mistyping a number so that the contract price or some other important detail is wrong. Section 8 of the Law Reform (Miscellaneous Provisions) (Scotland) Act 1985 now allows for correction of incorrectly expressed contracts, provided that third parties are not prejudiced by the correction.

In the second scenario, one of the parties may express himself incorrectly during pre-contractual negotiations; for example, a builder may make a mistake in the contract price when offering to carry out building work. The court will look at each case on its merits but if it is clear from prior negotiations that one party has simply expressed himself incorrectly in making an offer or an acceptance rather than making a mistake about the task itself then the court will allow reduction. For example, if the parties to a building contract had discussed how long a particular job was going to take and the builder said it would take 40 hours, he might make a mistake when writing this down on his offer to carry out the work and write "14 hours" instead. If the customer tried to take advantage of that error by accepting that offer uncorrected then the court may allow the contract to be reduced. However, if the builder had simply underestimated how long the job would take then it is unlikely that a court would reduce the contract on the basis of *that* error. (*Seaton Brick and Tile Co* v *Mitchell* (1900) and *Steel's Trustees* v *Bradley Homes (Scotland) Ltd* (1972).

(ii) Error of intention. A failure on the part of one or even both parties to realise the significance of a contract or the fact that it is legally binding will not usually affect the contract unless the error is essential and bilateral and therefore amounts to a lack of consensus.

Induced error – misrepresentation.

The courts are much more likely to find that the contract is affected by induced error. Induced error occurs when a misrepresentation of *fact* (ie not opinion) is made by one party which *induces* (makes) the other party enter into the contract. A misrepresentation must be made to that other party or to his agent and not simply be picked up from other sources or "heard through the grapevine". Trade puffs, adverts, opinions and hopes do not amount to misrepresentation. Misrepresentation falls into three categories:

(i) innocent misrepresentation;
(ii) fraudulent misrepresentation; and
(iii) negligent misrepresentation.

(i) Innocent misrepresentation. A misrepresentation is only innocent if the party who made it believes it to be true. If the misrepresentation goes to the heart of the contract then the contract will be void (again, because there is no *consensus in idem*). Other innocent misrepresentation can make the contract voidable and therefore open to challenge in the courts even if it is not an essential error (*Ritchie* v *Glass* (1936)). See below at Question (3) for a discussion of "essential error". If successful, the court would reduce (set aside) the contract. Reduction is possible only if three criteria are met:

(1) The misrepresentation is material. "Material" does not mean that it has to be an essential error in this context. To be material, the misrepresentation must be sufficiently important (a minor misrepresentation would not fulfil the next criteria).

(2) The misrepresentation was relied upon by the other party and induced him into the contract. This link between the misrepresentation and the existence of the contract is important.

(3) *Restitutio in integrum* must be possible, ie it must be possible to put the other party back into the position which he would have been in but for the contract. Innocent misrepresentation was discussed in the important cases of *Boyd & Forrest* v *Glasgow & South-Western Railway Co* (1912) and (the second action arising out of the same situation) *Boyd & Forrest* v *Glasgow & South-Western Railway Co* (1915) in which the contract could not be reduced (set aside) because *restitution* was not possible. These cases arose when Boyd & Forrest contracted with the railway company to do some work for a price based on figures supplied by the railway company. Unfortunately, those figures were wrong because they had been changed by an engineer (a genuine mistake). This meant that the actual cost of the work carried out by Boyd & Forrest was hugely more expensive than the agreed contract price. They claimed fraudulent misrepresentation (1912 action) but when no fraud was established they argued innocent misrepresentation (1915 action). Although this was proved, restitution was not possible because the route had been dynamited and could not be restored to its previous state. Boyd & Forrest lost out.

The general rule is that if reduction is not possible on these grounds then there is no other remedy for innocent misrepresentation and damages are not available. The exception to that rule is if the misrepresentation is actually incorporated in the contract itself (usually by including it as a written term). If the misrepresentation becomes a contractual term (and not just a pre-contractual term) and is found to be wrong then the party who relied on it may have a claim for damages (see Chapter 6).

Damages for misrepresentation which is not contractual in this way are limited to fraudulent and negligent misrepresentation (see below).

(ii) Fraudulent misrepresentation. Although there is no overarching duty of good faith in Scots contract law, if one party makes a fraudulent misrepresentation which induces the other party to enter into the contract then that can render the contract void or voidable.

If this type of error is essential then the contract is void through lack of consensus. If not, then the contract may be voidable and the rules for reduction are the same as for innocent misrepresentation. However, the innocent party may also claim damages in delict *even if* he cannot have the contract reduced.

How is fraudulent misrepresentation defined? The important English case of *Derry* v *Peek* (1889) was approved in the Scottish case of *Boyd & Forrest* v *Glasgow & South-Western Railway Co* (1912) and established the criteria for fraud:

- the person making the representation did not believe it to be true, or
- the person making the representation was *recklessly* careless as to whether it was true or false.

However, the Scottish Law Commission considers this to be too narrow a definition (SLC *Defective Consent and Consequential Matters*, Memo No 42, June 1978) and does not think that it would be followed today.

(iii) Negligent misrepresentation. Negligent misrepresentation can adversely affect a contract (*Esso Petroleum Co* v *Mardon* (1976)). Damages are available for negligent misrepresentation under s 10 of the Law Reform (Miscellaneous Provisions) (Scotland) Act 1985, which allows the innocent party to claim damages if he cannot have the contract reduced and has suffered a loss (provided that he can show that the other party owed him a duty of care).

(3) Is the error essential or not?

A number of essential errors – ie those which are classed as "going to the substantials" and which go right to the heart of the contract – have been established in Bell's *Principles* and case law.

Much of the confusion about the law of error stems from this classification. A logical approach to the law of error would suggest that all errors which can be classified as "essential" render the contract void. The law of error would then be a simple matter of checking whether a particular error or misunderstanding fell into the category of essential error and, if it did, finding that the contract was void as a result. The reality is much more complex, however, and the important thing to appreciate is that the mere classification of an error as essential does not automatically render a contract void. The effect on the contract can be deduced only by considering the answers to all three of the key questions: who made the error, how was it made and is it essential?

What errors are considered essential?

(a) Error as to subject matter. The parties or one of them may make a mistake about the subject matter of the contract, as in the case of *Raffles* v *Wichelhaus* (1864). In this case, the contract was for the sale and purchase of some cotton which was a cargo on board a ship called *Peerless*. Unfortunately, *Peerless* was a very common name for ships at the time and the buyers thought that they would be getting their cotton from a ship called *Peerless* due to sail from Bombay in October but the seller thought that the *Peerless* in question was the one sailing from Bombay in December. When the cotton arrived on the December ship, the buyers refused to take delivery of it and the sellers sued for payment. This was held to be an essential error and the contract was void through lack of consensus.

(b) Error as to identity of the parties. This is a very limited category. After all, when someone goes into a shop to buy a loaf of bread, all that usually matters is that the shopkeeper intends to sell the bread and the customer intends to buy; their respective identities are irrelevant. However, the case of *Morrisson* v *Robertson* (1908) demonstrates that there may be a particular characteristic of one party which is essential to the contract being made at all.

Morrisson entered into a contract to sell two cows to a man who told him that he was the son of a man whom Morrisson knew and who was of good character (and, more importantly in business, good credit). The cows were handed over on the understanding that the father would pay Morrisson on the usual credit terms. However, the "son" was in fact no relation of the father and the buyer was actually a rogue called Telford. By the time this was established, he had sold the cows on to an innocent third party and disappeared. This left Morrisson with neither cows nor payment and he sued the third party, Robertson, to get his cows back. If there had been a contract between Morrisson and Telford, then Telford would have been able to pass title (ownership) of the cows to Robertson and Morrisson would not have been able to get them back.

However, the court held that title had not passed to Telford because there had been no contract of sale between him and Morrisson. Morrisson had "contracted" on the basis that the buyer was the creditworthy father and the "son" was his agent. He was wrong. The contract was void. The recent English decision of *Shogun Finance Ltd* v *Hudson* (2004), which concerned fraudulent misrepresentation, also made the point that the identity of the customer is "fundamental" in consumer credit cases so this category of essential error may yet be relevant.

This contrasts with the case of *Macleod* v *Kerr* (1965) in which a seller of a car took payment in the form of a cheque from the purchaser which turned out to be stolen and bounced. By the time this was established, the purchaser had sold the car on to a third party. The seller argued that there had been an error of identity (ie if he had known that the purchaser was a thief then he would not have entered into the contract) and that the original contract to sell the car to him was void. The court disagreed. The purchaser did not pretend to be anyone other than himself and, although the contract was voidable because of the stolen cheque, the car could not be recovered from the third party because he had bought it in good faith and it was too late to prevent title from passing to him. The seller could, of course, take action against the purchaser to recover the price of the car – if he could find him!

(c) **Error as to price.** The parties may have different prices in mind when doing business and this may be essential. However, *Wilson* v *Marquis of Breadalbane* (1859) demonstrates that this will not always be considered essential. In this case, Wilson sold cows to the Marquis. Wilson thought the agreed price was £15 per cow but the Marquis thought the agreed price was £13 per cow and paid that amount. Although it seems clear that the parties had different ideas about the price, the court decided that there was a contract between them because they had acted upon it, ie the cows had been handed over in exchange for money. However, the court said that if the parties had not got as far as carrying out the contract, then it may have been decided differently.

(d) **Error as to quality, quantity or extent of the subject matter.** Error about quality is listed in Bell's *Principles* as an essential error but it seems unlikely that a contract would be reduced on this ground today unless the error was induced.

(e) **Error as to nature of contract.** *McLaurin* v *Stafford* (1875) and *Royal Bank of Scotland* v *Purvis* (1990) demonstrate that if one party makes a mistake about the legal effect of the contract then, provided that error is not induced by the other party, it does not amount to an essential error and so the contract is valid.

Effect of Essential Error. An essential error (even if uninduced) may render a contract void because it amounts to a lack of consensus which prevents the contract from being properly formed in the first place. However, this is not an automatic result of an error being classified as essential. The full answer to the question of the effect of error on a contract can only be given by putting all three elements of "who, how and what" together.

Thus, an incidental error which is not an essential error and is a more minor error will still affect the validity of the contract if it has been induced by misrepresentation.

Summary of effect of error

Uninduced unilateral error. *Effect*: this will usually not affect the contract unless it is essential *and* amounts to a lack of consensus or the contract is a gratuitous one.

Induced unilateral error. *Effect*: the contract is void (if it amounts to a lack of consensus) or voidable (even if the error is not essential).

Remedy: the correct remedy will depend on whether the misrepresentation is innocent, fraudulent or negligent. The parties may agree to set aside the contract (unlikely). Alternatively, where there has been innocent misrepresentation, the party who has been induced into the contract can apply to the court to have the contract set aside (reduced) but this will only be done if it can be shown that the misrepresentation is material (not necessarily essential), has induced the contract and that *restitution in integrum* is possible. Fraudulent and negligent misrepresentation also have the additional remedy of damages.

Bilateral error. *Effect*: if common and essential, then the contract is void due to a lack of consensus. If mutual and essential, then the contract is void but otherwise can only result in the contract being voidable if it is induced.

Remedy: if the contract is voidable then the parties can agree to reduce the contract, failing which, one of the parties can ask the court to reduce it.

(viii) Other prejudicial circumstances

There are other circumstances surrounding the formation of a contract which taint it. They concern the way in which one of the parties behaved in order to get the other to enter into the contract. These circumstances may render the contract void or voidable and include the following.

Facility and circumvention

Vulnerable people may retain capacity but be termed "facile" in law and be taken advantage of ("circumvention") by the other party in the contract. This is demonstrated by the case of *MacGilvray* v *Gilmartin* (1986) in which a mother asked the court to set aside a disposition (title deed of a house) which she had apparently granted in favour of her daughter voluntarily. The mother argued that shortly after being widowed she had been vulnerable and had signed a contract transferring ownership of her house to her daughter when asked to do so by her. She was therefore in a state of "facility" when she did this and her daughter had used this state of affairs to her own advantage. The mother was able to argue lesion, which means that she had been disadvantaged by this contract. She argued that it should be reduced on the grounds of facility and circumvention and/or undue influence. The court agreed that she was in a facile state when she signed the disposition and that her state had been taken advantage of. The disposition was set aside and ownership of the house reverted back to the mother. This case was followed in *Anderson* v *The Beacon Fellowship* (1992).

Undue influence

Undue influence is similar to facility and circumvention in that it involves one party taking advantage of another but the basis of the claim is different. In cases of undue influence, it is not that a person's facility is abused but rather that the other party abuses their own position of trust. These positions of trust can be familial, as in cases where a parent influences a child to make a decision which is not in his or her interest (*Gray* v *Binny* (1879)), or they can be found in cases of professional advisers who abuse their positions of trust to their own advantage. This happened in the case of *Honeyman's Executors* v *Sharp* (1978) in which a professional art adviser built up a relationship of trust with his client, only to use that influence to have her bequeath four valuable paintings to him in her will.

Force and fear

Consensus cannot exist where one party is threatened with or actually assaulted into agreeing to a contract. This is vividly demonstrated in the case of *Earl of Orkney* v *Vinfra* (1606) in which the Earl held a knife to his victim in order to convince him to sign over some property to him. This amounted to a lack of consent and the contract was void.

More subtle measures such as economic pressure have been discussed in cases like *Allen* v *Flood* (1898) and it has been held that as long as no unlawful means are used to back up such financial pressure then it is acceptable. Of course, one would need to look at the relationship between the parties to establish whether such pressure amounted to circumvention or undue influence.

Good faith

There is no overarching implied duty of good faith in the general law of contract in Scotland; each party negotiates a contract from the point of view of his own best interests. However, there are certain exceptions in which a duty of good faith will be implied and lack of good faith can affect whether the contract is valid.

(i) Contracts of utmost good faith

Very few contracts are contracts of utmost good faith (*uberrimae fidei*). These include partnership contracts and insurance contracts. The Marine Insurance Act 1906 applies to all forms of insurance contracts, despite its name, and contains a general duty of utmost good faith in s 17 which allows either party to avoid the contract (ie not fulfil their part of it) if the other breaches that duty. The 1906 Act also imposes two specific duties upon the assured (ie the party getting the insurance) which underpin that duty of utmost good faith:

(a) a duty of disclosure: the assured must disclose "every material circumstance" to the insurer (under s 18) (ie must not keep back important information relating to the contract); and

(b) avoid misrepresentation: every "material representation" made by the assured (or his agent) must be true (under s 20).

A breach of either duty allows the insurer to avoid the contract.

(ii) Cautionary obligations between spouses and banks

Cautionary obligations (ie contracts in which one party (the cautioner/ guarantor) agrees to pay sums due to a third party (the creditor) on behalf of another party (the debtor) if the debtor fails to do so) require that the parties to them act in good faith, at least in circumstances where the debtor and cautioner are husband and wife. The cases of *Barclays* v *O'Brien* (1994) and *Smith* v *Bank of Scotland* (1997) involved bank guarantees under which the wife of the debtor signed a guarantee which allowed the *family home* to be used to cover the husband's *business* debts to his creditor, the bank, should the husband fail to repay those debts. In each case, the husband did not repay his debts and the guarantee was called up by the bank, which would have meant that the family home would have to be sold to raise the money now due under the guarantee. In each case, the wife successfully challenged the contract of guarantee. The *Barclays* case is an English case and was decided on the basis that the husband had induced the wife into signing the guarantee by misrepresenting the nature of it to her. The court held that the wife should have received independent legal advice and refused to enforce the guarantee. The

Scottish courts reached the same outcome in *Smith* but on the different grounds of breach of good faith. The effect of these cases is that any spouse who intends to sign a guarantee for the business debts of the other spouse should be advised by the creditor (ie the bank) to get independent legal advice. The English case of *Royal Bank of Scotland* v *Etridge (No 2)* (2002) clarifies what is meant by "independent legal advice": a solicitor should explain to the guarantor spouse the nature of the document and its effects but need not satisfy himself that there is no undue influence (unless the circumstances suggest otherwise). However, the case of *Royal Bank of Scotland plc* v *Wilson* (2003) held that there is no authority that the specific rules of *Etridge* apply to Scotland.

It cannot be assumed that this implied duty will be extended to all cautionary obligations and only case law will tell.

(iii) Innocent and fraudulent misrepresentation

Although there is no overriding duty of good faith, this does not mean that there are no remedies available to one party if he has entered into a contract on the basis of a misrepresentation by the other. This is dealt with under error (above).

Essential Facts

- A contract which appears to have been formed may still have a problem which renders it void, voidable or unenforceable.

- A contract which is void is a contract which is so flawed that, although it was apparently formed and even acted upon, it was never a real contract.

- A contract which is voidable is one which has a problem which opens it up to challenge by one of the parties and can be set aside by a court. In contrast with a void contract, a voidable contract exists until the time it is set aside.

- A contract may be valid but the courts refuse to enforce it for another reason.

- The main problems which can affect contracts are: (1) lack of consensus, (2) lack of consent, (3) lack of capacity, (4) lack of formality where required, (5) illegality, (6) restrictions on freedom to contract, (7) error, and (8) facility and circumvention, undue influence, and lack of good faith where required.

Lack of consensus

- The parties must have consensus (agreement) about the main points of the contract for it to come into existence. Dissensus (lack of consensus) will render it void. Courts apply an objective test in deciding if there is consensus.

Lack of consent

- The parties must intend to create legal obligations. Social, domestic and gaming arrangements do not usually contain this consent to create legal obligations.
- This consent is usually implied in business arrangements but some pre-contractual negotiations can be excluded if circumstances (and not just words) show that there was no such intention.

Lack of capacity

- Both parties must have the capacity or legal ability to enter into the contract.
- The capacity of certain groups of persons is restricted in law. These include: children and young persons, adults with incapacity, intoxicated persons, registered companies, partnerships, unincorporated bodies and enemy aliens.
- Children and young persons: capacity is governed by the Age of Legal Capacity (Scotland) Act 1991. The general rule is that children aged under 16 have no contractual capacity and young persons aged 16 and over have full capacity. However, this is subject to certain exceptions. Children under 16 have capacity to enter into contracts of a type normal for their age: a child aged 12 and over may make a will; a child of sufficient understanding can consent to medical and similar treatment. Young persons aged 16 and 17 have further protection under the Act and can apply to the court to have any "prejudicial transaction" made at those ages set aside, provided they apply before the age of 21. This does not apply to contracts concluded in the course of the young person's business.
- Adults with incapacity: an adult who is vulnerable through mental illness, learning difficulty or dementia may have impaired capacity. The Adults with Incapacity (Scotland) Act 2000 makes provision for third parties to assume contractual capacity for that person under Power of Attorney, Guardianship Order or Intervention Order, as appropriate, primarily for medical and financial matters. Section 3(2) of the Sale of

Goods Act 1979 compels a person who cannot contract through mental incapacity to pay a reasonable price if he or she buys "necessaries".

- Intoxicated persons: a person has to be very drunk or high on drugs to lose capacity and if he or she does contract in that state then he or she must challenge the contract as soon as possible after sobering up. Drunkenness is also covered by s 3(2) of the Sale of Goods Act 1979.

- Registered companies: a registered company is a legal person and has capacity to contract. This will be limited only if its constitution limits what the company can and cannot do *and* the third party with whom the company is dealing knows about that limitation but contracts with the company in contravention of that limitation regardless (ss 35, 35A and 35B of the Companies Act 1985).

- Partnerships: partnerships have separate legal personality in Scotland (Partnership Act 1890, s 4). Partners can also enter into contracts on behalf of their firm but their authority to do that is limited by s 5 of the Partnership Act 1890.

- Unincorporated bodies: these are not separate legal persons and therefore do not have capacity to contract in their own right. They must contract through their office bearers.

- Enemy aliens: war affects capacity to enter into contracts.

Lack of formality

- Not all contracts have to be in writing to be valid. Those that do are listed in s 1 of the Requirements of Writing (Scotland) Act 1995. These are contracts relating to creation, transfer, variation or extinction of an interest in land (eg buying, selling and leasing houses, farms, factories and other real rights in land) and promises (except if given in the course of business). Tenancies or rights to occupy land for less than one year are exempted.

- A lack of formality can be cured if the circumstances of s 1(3) and (4) apply. These rules replace the old common law rules of homologation and *rei interventus.*

- If writing is required then it must be written (not electronic) and subscribed under s 2 of the 1995 Act.

- A contract can be made probative (self-proving) by attestation (witnessing) under s 3 of the 1995 Act or by being endorsed with a court certificate under s 4 of the 1995 Act.

- Persons who cannot sign their own contracts by reason of blindness, paralysis or other difficulty can have this done on their behalf by notarial execution under s 9 of the 1995 Act.

Illegality

- A contract formed for an illegal purpose is unenforceable (whether illegal on the face of it or not).

- A contract concluded for a legitimate purpose may be unenforceable if it is to be performed in an illegal way but this is not automatic, particularly if the illegality stems from breaches of legislation.

- Contracts illegal at common law include those contrary to public policy (eg criminal/sexual immorality/interfering with justice). The most common type of contract illegal at common law is the restraint of trade or restrictive covenant.

- Restraint of trade/restrictive covenants can be found in employment contracts, sale and purchase of business contracts and solus agreements. They attempt to restrict the rights of the other party to work/set up a new business or deal with any other supplier. They are unenforceable unless they protect legitimate business interests of the party seeking to enforce the covenant, are reasonable and in the public interest.

- The court will consider a range of issues including geographical and temporal limits, access to trade secrets and the general business environment in deciding if a restrictive covenant meets the criteria.

Restrictions on freedom to contract

- Be aware of other common law and legislation which restrict the parties' ability to agree certain terms. These include: (1) common law and exclusion clauses; (2) Unfair Contract Terms Act 1977; (3) Sale of Goods Act 1979; (4) Unfair Terms in Consumer Contracts Regulations 1999; (5) Consumer Credit Act 1974; and (6) Carriage of Goods By Sea Act 1992.

- Common law and exclusion clauses: courts not keen to enforce attempts to contract to exclude obligations or restrict liability. Such clauses are constructed *contra proferens* (against the party seeking to rely on them).

- Unfair Contract Terms Act 1977 (UCTA): this complex Act applies to many (but not all) contracts. It has five main effects: (1) it renders clauses which limit/exclude liability for death or personal injury arising out of breach of duty void; (2) it allows clauses which limit/exclude liability for other losses arising out of breach of duty *if* they are fair and reasonable; (3) it allows clauses in standard form or consumer contracts which limit/exclude liability for breach of contract *if* they are fair and reasonable; (4) it allows indemnity clauses in consumer contracts *if* fair and reasonable; and (5) it prohibits sellers of goods from excluding certain implied terms found in the Sale of Goods Act 1979 in contracts with consumers and allows such exclusions in other contracts *only if* fair and reasonable.
- Sale of Goods Act 1979: this Act implies certain terms into contracts for the sale of goods (The Supply of Goods (Implied Terms) Act 1973 does a similar job for hire goods.) There are implied terms about title (s 12), sale by description (s 13), quality and fitness for purpose (s 14) and sale by sample (s 15). Note the interrelation between Sale of Goods Act 1979 and UCTA.
- Unfair Terms in Consumer Contracts Regulations 1999: unlike UCTA, these Regulations only apply to terms in *consumer contracts* which have not been individually negotiated (ie standard form contracts) and the consumer must be a natural person. The Regulations do not allow "unfair terms" to be enforced against consumers. Unfair terms are those which cause a significant imbalance in the rights of the parties to the detriment of the consumer.
- Consumer Credit Act 1974: contracts for loans, overdrafts and credit cards between businesses and consumers are subject to certain restrictions under this Act.
- Carriage contracts: these contracts are subject to restrictions under Carriage of Goods legislation.

Error

- Contracting parties, or one of them, may have made a mistake when concluding the contract. The effect of that mistake on the validity of the contract is dealt with by the law of error.
- Error can lead to a lack of consensus in limited circumstances.
- Uninduced unilateral error (ie a mistake made by one of the parties without any inducement by anything the other party has said or done) will not usually affect the contract.

- In order to determine the effect of error on a contract, three questions need to be asked: (1) Who made the error? (2) What caused the error to be made? (3) Is it an essential error or not?

- Who made the error? If one party makes the mistake then, provided it is not induced by anything the other party said or did, this will not usually affect the contract. If both parties make a mistake, whether the same mistake (common error) or a different mistake (mutual error), then this is more likely to make the contract void through lack of consensus.

- What caused the error to be made? This is crucial in determining the effect of the mistake on the contract because induced error is much more likely to affect the validity of the contract. Induced error is also called misrepresentation. Misrepresentation can be innocent, fraudulent or negligent.

- Is it an essential error or not? This has less weight than it used to have but, nevertheless, if the error is not deemed essential then the contract is much less likely to be affected by it (but note overriding issue of inducement). Essential error is not definitively set out in case law but has been found to include error about the subject matter of the contract.

- Misrepresentation (induced error): innocent misrepresentation can lead to the contract being void (if lack of consensus) or voidable (even if not essential). If voidable, the court will only set aside (reduce) the contract if certain criteria can be met. These criteria are: (a) the misrepresentation is material (important but not necessarily essential); (b) the misrepresentation was relied upon by the other party and induced him into the contract;(c) *restitutio in integrum* must be possible, ie it must be possible to put the other party back into the position which he would have been in but for the contract.

- Misrepresentation (induced error): fraudulent misrepresentation occurs when the person making the representation does not believe it to be true or is reckless with the truth. Essential error makes the contract void in these circumstances. Non-essential error makes it voidable and the same criteria for setting aside (reduction) apply. In addition, damages in delict may be available even if contract cannot be set aside.

- Misrepresentation (induced error): negligent misrepresentation occurs if one party makes a representation negligently and the contract may be set aside by the court if the criteria can be met. If reduction is not possible then damages may be payable under s 10 of the Law Reform (Miscellaneous Provisions) (Scotland) Act 1985.

Other prejudicial circumstances

- Facility and circumvention: taking advantage of vulnerable person may render contract voidable (NB not the same as lack of capacity).
- Undue influence: similar but different – position of trust is abused.
- Force and fear: effect depends on level of and nature of methods used. Physical force = void through lack of consensus. Economic pressure = OK unless unlawful means used (eg blackmail).
- Good faith: no overarching duty of good faith but note specific problems of insurance contracts, partnership contracts, spousal guarantees and misrepresentation.

Essential Cases

Lack of consensus

Mathieson Gee (Ayrshire) Ltd v Quigley (1952): the pond case. One party thought the contract was for services and the other for equipment hire; no consensus, so no contract.

Lack of consent

Stobo Ltd v Morrisons (Gowns) Ltd (1949): pre-contractual negotiations in business case; court will look at all of the circumstances and not just the words of the parties to decide if consent is present.

Dawson International plc v Coats Paton plc (1988): breach of pre-contractual agreement case; court reached an equitable solution to allow one party to claim back money from the party in "breach".

Balfour v Balfour (1919): husband and wife case. Domestic arrangement did not imply consent to be legally bound.

Kelly v Murphy (1940) (and **Ferguson v Littlewoods Pools Ltd**) **(1997)**: gaming arrangements do not imply consent.

Robertson v Anderson (2003): bingo win causes friends to fall out. An agreement to share winnings did include consent to be legally bound, therefore enforceable contract in place.

Illegality

Barr v Crawford (1983): the publican and the bribes case; a contract of bribery in exchange for liquor licence renewal was prima facie illegal (illegal purpose) and unenforceable.

Pearce v Brooks (1866): prostitute's carriage case; although contract was prima facie for a legitimate purpose, the court found it was actually for an illegal purpose and unenforceable as both parties knew what the carriage was to be used for.

Dowling & Rutter v Abacus Frozen Foods Ltd (No 2) (2002): performance of supply of labour contract performed illegally because it breached immigration legislation; however, court allowed it to be enforced (lack of knowledge a factor).

Bluebell Apparel Ltd v Dickinson (1978): jeans restrictive covenant case; manufacturer of Wranglers entitled to enforce restrictive covenant preventing ex-employee going to work for Levis as he had access to trade secrets which the company had legitimate right to protect.

Stewart v Stewart (1899): photographer restrictive covenant – 20-mile restriction around Elgin was enforceable.

Dallas McMillan & Sinclair v Simpson (1989): restrictive covenant where 20-mile radius around Glasgow Cross not enforceable.

Mulvein v Murray (1908): "blue pencil" case; severable clauses can be saved if some reasonable but others not – court will delete unreasonable parts.

Nordenfelt v Maxim Nordenfelt Guns and Ammunition Co Ltd (1894): the ultimate restraint – 25 years, worldwide but still enforceable in the circumstances.

Dumbarton Steamboat Co Ltd v Macfarlane (1899): the purchaser of a business operating in the West Coast of Scotland only could not impose a UK-wide ban on its seller.

Esso Petroleum Co Ltd v Harpers Garages (Stourport) Ltd (1968): 21-year solus agreement too long.

Error

Stewart v Kennedy (1890): an essential error, provided it is not induced by the other party, does not invalidate a written onerous contract.

Spook Erection (Northern) LW v Kaye (1990): 99-year lease case. One party made a mistake, thinking that property affected by 990-year lease. Court said: too bad – contract stands. NB error was uninduced.

Hunter v Bradford Property Trust (1970): errors in gratuitous contracts are more likely adversely to affect the contract.

Steuart's Trustees v Hart (1875): if one party makes an uninduced error and the other finds out but keeps quiet and takes advantage of that mistake, then there is more likelihood of contract being void or voidable. Approved in *Angus* v *Bryden*.

Hamilton v Western Bank (1861): common essential error renders contract void.

Ritchie v Glass (1936): induced error through innocent misrepresentation can render contract voidable even if not an essential error.

Boyd & Forrest v Glasgow & South-Western Railway Co (1912, 1915): the "wrong kind of railway costings" case which spawned two actions: one for fraudulent misrepresentation (1912) and one for innocent misrepresentation (1915). Engineer made genuine mistake in figures, leading to big increase in bill. However, restitution not possible as route already dynamited.

Derry v Peek (1889): English case setting out test for fraudulent misrepresen-tation.

Esso Petroleum Co v Mardon (1976): negligent misrepresentation can adversely affect contract.

Raffles v Wichelhaus (1864): *Peerless* case – essential error over which ship to be used for cargo rendered contract void through lack of consensus.

Morrisson v Robertson (1908): classic identity case. Essential error rendered contract void when Morrisson thought he was selling cows to a party representing a man whom he knew to have a good credit history but was duped in this. Contrast with *Macleod* v *Kerr*. Note *Shogun*.

Macleod v Kerr (1965): cars, not cows, identity case. The error was not essential here because the seller of the car entered into contract with *a* purchaser – it did not matter to him who the purchaser was, unlike the *Morrisson* case. However, when purchaser turned out to be a cheat, court said contract voidable because of the fraud; but this came too late as car by then sold on to third party acting in good faith.

Wilson v Marquis of Breadalbane (1859): error as to price not always essential.

McLaurin v Stafford (1875) (and **Royal Bank v Purvis) (1990)**: error about legal nature of contract not essential (although effect will change if error induced).

Other prejudicial circumstances

MacGilvary v Gilmartin (1986): facility and circumvention case; widowed old lady taken advantage of by daughter to get hands on house deeds; contract voidable and deeds signed back to mother.

Gray v Binny (1879): undue influence case in which mother influenced son to make a bad bargain over his inheritance.

Honeyman's Executors v Sharp (1978): undue influence case involving professional adviser.

Earl of Orkney v Vinfra (1606): force and fear case – sign contract or be stabbed. Void.

Allen v Flood (1898): economic pressure not force and fear unless un-lawful.

Barclays v O'Brien (1994): English spousal guarantee case – husband misrepresented nature of contract to wife therefore guarantee for his business debts not enforced.

Smith v Bank of Scotland (1997): same result for different reason – breach of good faith. Spouses should get independent legal advice.

Royal Bank of Scotland v Etridge (No 2) (2002): specific rules on what is meant by "independent legal advice", although doubt cast on whether these apply to Scotland in *Wilson*.

4 CONTRACTUAL TERMS

A contract can contain many different terms and the purpose of this chapter is, first, to identify how contractual terms are incorporated into contracts; second, to define these terms; and, third, to examine how courts will apply the rules of construction in order to interpret a contract.

INCORPORATION

How do we know which terms are included in a contract and which are not? The terms of a contract may be express or implied but they must be properly incorporated (ie included) in the contract to have effect. The general rule is that a contractual term cannot be incorporated into the contract after the contract has been made. The exception to this rule is if the parties agree to vary the terms of the contract. Contractual terms must be brought to the attention of the other party and the more unusual or onerous the term is, the more the party who wants to rely on it must do to bring it to the attention of the other party (*Spurling* v *Bradshaw* (1956) and *Interfoto Picture Library Ltd* v *Stiletto Visual Programmes Ltd* (1988)).

Questions about proper incorporation have arisen in a number of situations.

Ticket cases

Tickets for travel, car parking or other services may state that they are "subject to terms and conditions". Are those terms and conditions, which the purchaser may never see, contractual (ie part of the contract and enforceable as such)? The rules which have developed, to answer this question, are:

(a) If the ticket itself is part of the contract then the terms and conditions referred to in it are also contractual. The following are contractual:
- rail tickets.

The following are not contractual and therefore any terms referred to in them are not contractual:
- receipts (*Taylor* v *Glasgow Corporation* (1952)): a case in which a customer at public baths was issued with a receipt for her payment to enter the baths which evidenced that she had paid for it and entitled her to have a bath on presenting it to an attendant. This receipt/voucher was non-contractual;
- invoices (*Buchanan & Co* v *Macdonald* (1895)).

(b) The ticket must give adequate notice of the terms and conditions. The following may prevent incorporation of the terms:

- tiny print (*Williamson* v *North of Scotland and Orkney Steam Navigation Co* (1916);

- referring to the terms and conditions on the back of the ticket. However, in the case of *Parker* v *South-Eastern Railway Co* (1877), the fact that the front of the ticket did state "see back" was enough to incorporate the terms on the back of the ticket into the contract.

(c) The terms must be referred to before or during conclusion of the contract and not afterwards. In *Thornton* v *Shoe Lane Parking Ltd* (1971) a motorist parked in a car park, having received his ticket from an automatic ticket machine. The ticket stated: "This ticket is subject to the conditions of issue as displayed on the premises." The notice containing those conditions was not visible when Mr Thornton bought the ticket. The court held that the contract was concluded when Mr Thornton put his money into the automatic ticket machine so the ticket was post-contractual.

Notices

Notices are usually used to try to exclude or limit liability. Chapter 3 deals with the validity or otherwise of such exclusion/limitation clauses. However, even although UCTA applies to both contractual terms and non-contractual notices, it does not operate to turn notices into contractual terms and so it is still necessary to look at whether the notice is actually contractual or not. Furthermore, the notice may refer to other (non-exclusion/limitation) terms which are not covered by UCTA and so it is necessary to decide if it is contractual or not.

Again, the rules of incorporation apply to establish if a notice has been properly incorporated. In particular, the notice must be incorporated before or during conclusion of the contract and not afterwards. In the case of *Olley* v *Marlborough Court Ltd* (1949), a couple booked into a hotel and went up to their bedroom. A notice hung in the bedroom which purported to exclude liability for guests' articles being lost or stolen from the hotel. It was held that this notice was post-contractual and therefore not part of the contract. Any terms on it could not be enforced.

TERMS

There are a number of different types of terms in a contract.

(i) Classification

Conditions

Contracts create obligations between the parties to it. For example, a contract of lease between a landlord and a tenant creates certain obligations between them. The landlord is obliged to allow the tenant to live at the property and the tenant is obliged to pay rent. The tenant may be obliged to take care of the property and to pay for breakages. The landlord may be obliged to ensure that the property is furnished and so on. However, the mere creation of these obligations is not enough – the parties need to know *when* they have to fulfil the obligations. The timing of performance of an obligation may depend on a particular date being set such as the stipulation that rent is due on the first day of each calendar month. Timing of performance may depend on the other party doing something first: for example, the contract between the landlord and tenant may be concluded on the basis that the landlord will refit the kitchen before the tenant moves in and the tenant will be allowed to move in 7 days after that has been done. The contract may oblige the landlord to refit the kitchen by a certain date. The obligation to pay for breakages will have to be fulfilled only if something covered by this clause is actually broken. The contract may state that it will be terminated if the tenant sub-lets the property to anyone without the landlord's approval or the property is damaged by an Act of God. Each of these stipulations about timing of performance is a "condition". Conditions can be further broken down into different categories:

Contingent. The condition which triggers performance is not certain but depends on something else happening first. For example, the tenant is obliged to pay for a breakage only if it happens; the tenant may never break the landlord's plates etc and so the tenant may never have to fulfil that particular obligation. The lease will terminate if the tenant sub-lets without agreement. Again, he may or may not ever do that. Thus, a contingent condition can be *suspensive*, as in the case of the breakages, meaning that it may or may not ever trigger performance of the obligation (ie the obligation to pay for breakages). Alternatively, a contingent condition may be *resolutive* as in the case of the sub-letting clause because the obligation to pay rent and the landlord's obligation to allow tenancy *ends* if a particular trigger occurs.

Future. A condition is future if it is not dependent on an event which may or may not happen but on an event that *will* happen. Thus, the obligation to pay rent on the first day of each month is a future condition because the first day of the month is not a potential occurrence but a definite one. It simply means that the landlord has to wait until that time for the obligation to pay rent to be fulfilled and cannot call upon the tenant to fulfil it sooner.

Potestative. This is a condition which is within the control of one of the parties to the contract to fulfil. Thus, the obligation on the tenant to move in and on the landlord to allow tenancy is contingent on the landlord refitting the kitchen, which is within the landlord's control.

Casual. A casual condition is one which is subject to a chance occurrence or the actions of a third party (ie neither the landlord nor the tenant). The obligation to pay for breakages is casual because it is based on a chance occurrence. Termination due to Act of God such as lightning, flood or storm damage would be casual.

Mixed. This category of condition is a mix of potestative and casual parts.

Express terms

A contract term is express when it is stated: eg the price of a loaf of bread is a contract term and is express because of the price label on the shelf. A contract for purchasing land will expressly state the name of the property, the price, date of entry and so on. A contract term may be expressed verbally or in writing.

If the parties have made a mistake in expressing the written terms they can apply to the court to have the contract rectified under ss 8 and 9 of the Law Reform (Miscellaneous Provisions) (Scotland) Act 1985. A promise can also be rectified in this way.

Implied terms

A contract term is implied if it is not express but nonetheless forms part of the contract. It may be implied by statute, as in many cases of consumer protection legislation such as the Sale of Goods Act 1979 which implies contractual terms to the effect that goods sold in the course of business are of satisfactory quality etc.

A contract term may be implied by the common law: eg there is an implied duty of care owed by solicitors to their clients and an implied duty on the part of employees under a contract of employment to exercise due care and skill when doing their job.

A contract term may be implied by the customary practices in a particular trade but this is very limited. For example, the case of *The Moorcock* (1889) concerned a contract between a wharf owner and a ship owner under which the ship was to be docked at the wharf. In docking, the ship was damaged by the poor surface of the riverbed below. The court held that there was an implied term that the wharf owner would take reasonable care to ensure that the riverbed was safe for the ship to dock there.

There is some debate about whether certain terms can be implied "generally", such as the obligation to perform contractual obligations within a reasonable period of time (see McBryde, para 9.13, MacQueen and Thomson, para 3.34).

The courts will apply the "business efficacy test" to imply terms to make sense of a commercial transaction but only if it is reasonable to do so (*McWhirter* v *Longmuir* (1948) and *Lothian* v *Jenolite* (1969)).

Warranties

A warranty is a statement of fact in a contract and will usually be express. Contracts for the sale and purchase of a business, for example, often begin with a long list of facts about the business which are "warranted" by the seller such as turnover, number of staff, property holdings and so on.

Warranties can also be implied by law: for example, s 39 of the Marine Insurance Act 1906 implies a warranty of seaworthiness in a particular type of marine insurance contract.

In the general law of contract, a warranty carries no more weight than any other term in the contract; although this is not the case in insurance contracts, in which breach of warranty automatically terminates the contract (*Bank of Nova Scotia* v *Hellenic Mutual War Risks Association (Bermuda) Ltd (The Good Luck)* (1992)).

Written terms

If the contract is in writing then the presumption is that the document(s) contain all of the contractual terms and conditions. However, s 1(1) and (2) of the Contract (Scotland) Act 1997 allow additional evidence from outwith the written document to be brought to show that there were other terms and conditions unless the contract states that this is not permitted (s 1(3)). This additional evidence is called parole evidence and might be evidence of conversations between the parties or other documents which add to the written contract. If the contract contains a clause which states that all of the terms of the contract are to be found in the contract itself, then that is called a "whole contract clause" and parole evidence cannot be used.

(ii) Specific types of clauses in contracts

A written contract is made up of a number of clauses, some of which will deal with the key provisions of the agreement such as price, delivery dates, quantity of goods and so on; others are more general and are called "boilerplate clauses". A number of common boilerplate clauses are discussed below.

Arbitration clause

Although it is not legal in the general law of contract to attempt to restrict one party from using the courts as a legitimate forum for settling disputes if things go wrong between the parties, it is possible for the parties to agree on a form of alternative dispute resolution in the contract and they will then be bound to use that method first. If the method chosen in the contract is arbitration, then any arbitration award is binding on the parties. Arbitration is a popular method of dispute resolution in certain industries.

However, arbitration clauses are, prima facie, unfair in consumer contracts under Sch 2(q) to the Unfair Terms in Consumer Contracts Regulations 1999. Note also that, under arbitration law, the Regulations are extended to cover both legal and natural persons for this purpose and arbitration agreements for modest amounts (currently set at up to £5,000) are deemed unfair under the Regulations and therefore are not enforceable against consumers (Arbitration Act 1996, ss 89–91 and Unfair Arbitration Agreements (Specified Amounts) Order 1999).

Assignation clause

An assignation clause sets out whether one or both of the parties is entitled to assign (transfer) his part of the contract to a third party and, if so, whether the consent of the other party is required.

Choice of law and jurisdiction clause

A choice of law and jurisdiction clause states which country's laws are to be used in interpreting and applying the contract (choice of law) and which country's court system will be used to resolve any disputes (jurisdiction). This will be relevant in cross-border contracts in which the parties are in different countries. It is relevant even in contracts which are formed and performed within the UK as, of course, there are three separate jurisdictions to choose from (Scotland, England and Wales, Northern Ireland). A large company based in London which contracts with customers all over the UK may state in its contracts that the English courts will have jurisdiction and that English law will apply. If there is no jurisdiction clause or it is disputed then the Civil Jurisdiction and Judgments Act 1982 applies to determine jurisdiction. If there is no choice of law clause (or if it is to be disputed) then the Contracts (Applicable Law) Act 1990 applies to determine choice of law. This Act is discussed in more detail in Chapter 8.

Exclusion clause

An exclusion clause is a type of exemption clause. Exclusion clauses are an attempt by one party to exclude liability for an obligation which he would otherwise be bound by and thereby avoiding liability for not fulfilling that obligation: eg "The seller accepts no liability for the failure to deliver the goods on time" and "Park here at your own risk. Liability is excluded for all damage to vehicles." These are subject to both common law and statutory controls (UCTA) (see Chapter 3).

Force majeure

The law of frustration allows contracts to be terminated by certain events which make performance of the contract impossible. The parties to a contract may want to specify which events will allow one or both to terminate the contract or limit performance in some way. This is usually limited to events like natural disasters (or "Acts of God"), fire, flood, strikes, riots and so on, as long as none is caused by the parties (see Chapter 7).

Indemnity clause

One party may want the other to indemnify him, in the event that the former loses out in some way as a result of the performance of the contract. For example, if one party is appointed as the agent for another and undertakes to carry out certain tasks for that party (the principal) then the contract between them may state that the principal is to reimburse all reasonable expenses and costs incurred by the agent in performing that contract (ie carrying out those tasks for the principal). A contract for car hire may require the customer to reimburse the car hire company for any loss arising out of the contract of hire. As noted in Chapter 3, s 18 of UCTA does restrict the use of these clauses in consumer contracts.

Interpretation clause

A contract may use a number of key words and, rather than risk problems with construction of those key words, they will actually be listed and defined in the contract's interpretation clause. For example, a contract for the sale of goods may define key words such as "buyer", "goods", "place of delivery", "price" and "seller" in its interpretation clause.

Limitation clause

A limitation clause is another type of exemption clause. A limitation clause attempts to cap the liability of one of the parties for breach of duty or contract by setting a monetary limit on liability or limiting the time limit allowed for claims (note that prescription, which limits the time for making claims, is also covered by statute – see Chapter 7). See Chapter 3 for a discussion on the enforceability of limitation clauses.

CONSTRUCTION

Construction concerns the way in which the courts interpret the terms of a contract which may be ambiguous or the matter of dispute between the parties. Even the most careful draftsman of contracts may find that the wording of a contract can be interpreted by each of the parties differently or may have to be interpreted to apply to a situation which was not contemplated at the time of drafting. The courts are not inclined to do the parties' jobs for them and to renegotiate and redraft contracts so that they are better. If the parties disagree on how a term is to be interpreted then the courts will use the following rules of construction to find a meaning.

Ordinary meaning of words

The general rule is that the words used in the contract should be interpreted literally and given their ordinary meaning within the context of the whole contract. This approach does not take into account the intention of the parties, except to the extent that this is evident within the contract itself.

In cases where this test is not sufficient to establish one outright meaning of a word or phrase then the Scottish courts will consider some evidence from outwith the contract (*Inglis* v *Buttery & Co* (1878)). This does not extend to pre-contractual negotiations but only to circumstances around the time of formation itself. In other words, the courts will look at only a very limited range of external factors if the word is still ambiguous.

However, this strict objective rule has been modified in English law to some extent, with judges placing the words in the context of the whole contract *and* "the background knowledge which would have been available to the parties in the situation which they were at the time of the contract" (per Lord Hoffmann, *Investors Compensation Scheme Ltd* v *West Bromwich Building Society* (1998) at p 912). Lord Hoffmann called these the "common sense principles". This does not go so far as to mean that the courts will take into account evidence of pre-contractual negotiations or what each party thought the words would mean because that would change it from an objective to a subjective test, but it does allow the court to decide that a purely literal interpretation of the words is not what the "reasonable man" would take the words to mean.

It is not clear whether the Scottish courts will adopt this approach (MacQueen and Thomson, para 3.44).

Technical meaning of words

If a word has a technical meaning then that meaning will be used, unless it is clear from the contract that the ordinary meaning, if there is one, should be used. Technical words could include terms from a particular industry or they could have a technical meaning in law.

Contra proferentem rule

This rule will usually be used in contracts which have been drafted by one of the parties, such as insurance contracts, pre-printed terms and conditions of trading and the like. The court will interpret any ambiguous word or phrase against (ie *contra*) the party who has put it forward (ie the *proferens*), and who will therefore want to rely on it having a particular meaning, if that meaning prejudices the other party.

Eiusdem generis rule

This rule applies to lists which state a number of specific items, activities or purposes and conclude with some general words like "and other such items" or "and other such activities".

For example, an insurance contract may state that "all necklaces, bracelets, rings, watches and other valuables shall be listed and insured separately". If the assured's state of the art camera is stolen and is not separately insured, the assured will argue that it is not covered by the phrase "other valuables" and the insurance company will argue that it is. The *eiusdem generis* rule will be applied if the specific listed items all fall into one group (*genus*), in which case the general words apply to include only things in the same group. The question thus becomes: "Is the camera a valuable belonging to the same group as the jewellery and watches?" Although valuable, it does not fall into the same group and so would not have to be listed and separately insured.

The case of *Abchurch Steamship Co* v *Stinnes* (1911) is authority for the point that there must be an identifiable genus for this rule to apply.

Essential Facts

- Contracts are not always contained in concise documents. The rules of incorporation may have to be applied to determine which are contractual terms and which are not.

- The terms of a contract may be express or implied but they must be properly incorporated (ie included) in the contract to have effect.
- The general rule is that a contractual term cannot be incorporated into a contract after that contract has been made. The exception to this rule is if the parties agree to vary the terms of the contract.
- Contractual terms must be brought to the attention of the other party and, the more unusual or onerous the term is, the more the party who wants to rely on it must do to bring it to the attention of the other party.
- Tickets and notices pose particular problems in ascertaining if terms on or referred to in them are properly incorporated into the contract. Some tickets are definitely contractual: eg rail tickets. Receipts are issued post-contract and cannot therefore include contractual terms.
- The terms of the contract can fall into different categories: conditions (contingent, future, potestative and casual), express terms, implied terms, warranties, written and non-written terms.
- If a contract is in writing, then it is presumed to contain all terms unless parole evidence is permitted under the Contract (Scotland) Act 1997.
- Some common clauses in contracts are: arbitration, assignation, choice of law and jurisdiction, exclusion, *force majeure*, indemnity, interpretation and limitation clauses.
- The rules of construction allow courts to interpret ambiguous or disputed terms in contracts. The rules of construction are that words will usually be given their ordinary meaning; technical words will be given their technical meaning; ambiguous words or phrases will be interpreted contra or against the party putting them forward; and the *eiusdem generis* rule may apply to some lists.

Essential Cases

Spurling v Bradshaw (1956): the more unusual or onerous a term is, the more effort has to be made to draw the other party's attention to it.

Taylor v Glasgow Corporation (1952): swimming baths receipt/voucher issued after contract made not able to incorporate contractual terms.

Buchanan & Co v Macdonald (1895): invoices issued after contract cannot incorporate contractual terms.

Williamson v North of Scotland and Orkney Steam Navigation Co (1916): tiny print may prevent incorporation.

Parker v South-Eastern Railway Co (1877): "See back" printed on front of ticket was enough to incorporate terms on back.

Thornton v Shoe Lane Parking Ltd (1971): car park, ticket and notice case. Ticket referring to notice issued after contract made and notice not visible at time contract made.

Olley v Marlborough Court Ltd (1949): notice in hotel bedroom post-contractual and not incorporated.

The Moorcock (1889): rare case of contractual terms being implied by customary practice in a trade.

McWhirter v Longmuir (1948) and **Lothian v Jenolite (1969)**: business efficacy test will be applied in constructing terms of contract if reasonable to do so.

Bank of Nova Scotia v Hellenic (The Good Luck) (1992): insurance warranties have particular importance and breach of these terminates the contract.

Abchurch Steamship Co v Stinnes (1911): application of *eiusdem generis* rule to a list with an identifiable genus (group of related items/ activities/etc).

5 THIRD PARTY RIGHTS

Most contracts are between two parties, which means that each of them (but no one else) gets certain rights under that contract and must perform certain obligations under it; this is called privity of contract. Someone who is not party to the contract – a third party – can never have any obligations under the contract imposed upon him. Similarly, a third party would not normally get any rights under that contract. However, these are general rules and there are three main exceptions:

(1) agency;
(2) assignation; and
(3) *ius quaesitum tertio.*

AGENCY

An agent enters into a contract on behalf of his principal. The contractual rights and obligations are therefore between the principal and the party with whom the agent made the contract on his behalf (provided that the agent has acted within his authority).

ASSIGNATION OF RIGHTS

A third party can also obtain rights (and obligations if he agrees) under a contract if he agrees to an assignation of the rights due to one party under the contract in his favour. For example, in partnership law, a third party who is not a partner in the firm and therefore not party to the partnership agreement can receive a right to the share of profits of one partner if that partner's share is assigned to him under s 31 of the Partnership Act 1890. Similarly, one party to a contract may assign his right to receive payment under that contract to a third party in settlement of a debt he owes to that third party. The book debts of businesses (ie a list of money owed to the business and due to be paid) can be used in this way as collateral for bank loans (note interrelationship with law of securities too).

Assignation is allowed only if the contract provides for it or, if not, the other party agrees.

Assignation of rights and duties

It is possible for the whole of one party's part of the contract (rights *and* duties) to be transferred to another party. For example, if A buys B's business,

then B will transfer all of the contracts which B's business is to perform to
A. A will then have to perform the contracts and will receive any benefits
due under the contracts. It is a full substitution of A for B. There is some
discussion about whether this type of transfer should be called assignation or
delegation. (See Chapter 7 for discussion of delegation.)

The important distinction is not so much in the name because assignation
is currently in common usage for both transfers; the important thing to
know is *what* is being transferred and the effect of that on the original
contracting party, the assignor. If it is just the rights, then the assignor is still
a party to the contract and has to fulfil any outstanding obligations under it.
If it is everything (ie a full substitution), then the assignor steps out of the
contract and is no longer liable for any obligations under it (subject to any
agreement between the parties).

IUS QUAESITUM TERTIO

A third party can acquire legally enforceable rights under this rule. The
following criteria are needed for *ius quaesitum tertio* to exist:

(a) the third party must be identified in the contract (*Finnie* v *Glasgow
and South-Western Railway Co* (1857)) (the third party can be named
personally or he can belong to a class or group of persons which is
referred to in the contract) *and*

(b) the parties who are entering into the contract must intend to benefit
that third party *and*

(c) that intention must be irrevocable (the parties to the contract cannot
then change their minds and take the intended right away from the
third party). This point is controversial. How do the parties make the
intention to confer a right irrevocable?

   (i) The parties may register the contract in the Books of Council
and Session which are public records.

   (ii) The parties to the contract could inform the third party of the
right.

   (iii) The third party could rely on the right.

   (iv) The term granting the right could state its irrevocability

(MacQueen and Thomson, para 2.77.)

Life assurance contracts are often quoted as examples of *ius quaesitum
tertio* in action: the assured takes out a policy with an insurer, naming a third
party as beneficiary of the policy. The third party therefore receives a right
to the amount of life cover taken out by the assured.

Essential Facts

- A contract is usually enforceable only between the two parties to it but third parties can acquire rights and/or obligations under the contract in certain circumstances: agency, assignation and *ius quaesitum tertio* (IQT).

- Agency is the relationship whereby one, the agent, acts on behalf of another, the principal, in entering into contracts. The principal has the rights/obligations under the contract even although the agent entered into it for him.

- Assignation: the rights or the rights and obligations may be assigned by one party to another and the assignee then has an enforceable right and/or obligations under the contract.

- IQT confers a benefit on a third party not a party to the contract if the third party is named, there is an intention to create an obligation in his favour and it is irrevocable.

6 BREACH OF CONTRACT

Many students of Scots law find breach of contract difficult: it is not helped by the fact that the key words used in breach of contract are sometimes used in different ways by different judges and academic writers. However, a question on breach of contract can usually be broken down into two key questions:

- What type of breach is it?
- What is the remedy for that breach?

This chapter will focus on answering those two key questions but first it is necessary to consider the role of breach of contract. What is it for?

The first point to note about breach of contract is that it is about *performance* of the contract rather than a problem with the contract itself. Previous chapters have discussed how contracts are formed and the problems which may occur if certain key elements are lacking or the terms of the contract are difficult to interpret or the contract contains clauses which are frowned upon in law. However, breach of contract is something else altogether: breach of contract is concerned with a failure to perform one's obligations under the contract or to do so properly or on time. Each of the parties will have certain obligations under the contract and they will usually have agreed when those obligations are to be performed (due date for performance). Examples of behaviour which can amount to breach of contract include the following:

- Failing to pay the contract price on time. The contract price will be the amount of money due to be paid by one party to the other for the goods, services, rent, etc when it falls due. The contract will usually specify a time for payment and that is the due date for performance of that obligation.
- Failure to deliver goods ordered under the contract.
- Failure to deliver the correct goods (eg a garden centre business which orders 3,000 lavender bushes from its supplier will not be pleased if 3,000 rose bushes are delivered instead).
- Failure to deliver the goods at the right time.
- Failure to perform the service required by the contract (eg a painter and decorator contracted to redecorate an office suite fails to turn up to paint the office as agreed, or a hire car booked for a holiday is not

available when the customer goes to collect it, or a singer booked to
perform at a concert refuses to perform).

- Failure to perform service adequately (eg painter decorates office suite
  but does a terrible job).

- Failure to perform services in conformity with contract (eg the singer
  does turn up to perform but, instead of singing opera as agreed, sings
  country and western songs).

- One party tells the other that he will not be performing his obligations
  at all.

- A fact stated in the contract and which induced the contract turns
  out to be wrong (misrepresentation – see Chapter 3).

In each case, the party who is not in breach (known as the "innocent" or
"aggrieved" party) will want to do something about it; he will want to seek
a remedy. He can select from a menu of options but the exact choice will
depend on the type of breach.

TYPES OF BREACH

Breaches of contract fall into three main situations:

(1) Repudiation/anticipatory breach

Repudiation occurs when one of the parties declares that he will not fulfil his
part of the contract (either before, on or after the due date for performance)
and this declaration is accepted by the innocent party. Repudiation is always
a material breach of contract (see below for a discussion of materiality). The
innocent party's acceptance of the refusal is sometimes referred to as
"rescission" but it simply has the same effect as rescission (see below for a
discussion of rescission).

   If the refusal to perform is declared before the due date for performance
then that is an anticipatory breach. If the refusal takes place on or after the
due date for performance then that is an ordinary breach. It is important to
know the difference between the two as this can affect the remedies available
to the innocent party.

   It is easy to confuse this category of breach (repudiation) with category
(2) (late/non-performance). The key to understanding repudiation is to
appreciate the fact that the party in breach is actually refusing to carry out
his part of the contract rather than simply being late in doing so. It is also
important to note the role of the innocent party in its creation.

For example, if two parties have entered into a contract whereby A will buy B's house, the contract will set out the date of entry, the price and other important matters such as whether the fridge, dishwasher and carpets are included in the sale. At its most basic, the seller is undertaking to vacate the house on the agreed date of entry and transfer ownership of it to the buyer on that date and in return the buyer is undertaking to pay the price on that day. What happens if the seller phones the buyer on the date of entry and says that he has changed his mind and no longer wants to sell the house but intends to stay put? As we have seen, cancellation rights only apply to a small class of contracts and this is not one of them.

The buyer has two options:

(a) he can accept the seller's repudiation and the contract is thereby repudiated and terminates. The buyer can then choose from the remedies available for repudiation; or

(b) he can refuse to accept the seller's position: the contract would not be repudiated and would continue because the buyer has thereby affirmed it. If the seller did then carry out his threat not to perform and did not move out or sign over ownership of the house to him, the buyer would seek the remedies also available for late/non-performance.

The buyer's response in the sequence of events is therefore important because it does two things: it affects the nature of the breach and consequently affects the nature of the remedies which can be sought for that breach. In making the decision on how to react, the buyer really needs to think about what he wants to achieve at the end of the day. Does he want to push for possession of the house or does he want to end the contract and claim back any legal fees, removal van cancellation costs and the like which he may have incurred as a result of entering into and acting upon the contract?

If answering a problem question on this, it is important to look at the sequence of events between the parties. It is unlikely that either party would ever use the correct legal terminology in their discussions in a matter like this and so any student of contract must be able to label each exchange in the sequence of events in order to give legal advice. For example, using the house sale scenario, the seller would probably not say, "I'm repudiating this contract", but he might say, "The deal's off – I'm not going anywhere!" How does one advise the buyer?

• Advice to the buyer would have to label that behaviour as a refusal to perform the contract.

- The buyer must then consider how to respond. Does he want to accept that refusal thereby turning the seller's action into repudiation which terminates the contract, or not?
- The decision will depend on what remedy the buyer wants to seek (see below for remedies): ie what is his desired outcome?

(2) Late performance (also known as non-performance)

Late performance occurs when one of the parties does not perform his obligations on time (whether that is to do something such as to deliver goods on time or to pay the contract price on time). Unlike repudiation, there is no actual *refusal* to perform – just a failure to perform when performance is due. Looking at the house sale example, the seller might still intend to move out and transfer ownership but phones the buyer to say that "I just haven't had the time to get organised". The due date for performance is the date of entry but it passes without him fulfilling his obligations under the contract by moving out and transferring ownership to the buyer. The first question that has to be answered is "Is this a material breach?" Materiality will determine what remedies are available and, once more, the buyer has to make a decision about how to respond.

(3) Defective performance

Defective performance occurs when one party does perform his obligations under the contract but does so defectively and therefore not in a manner acceptable to the other party. Defective performance often arises in two types of contract: sale of goods contracts and building contracts. In a sale of goods contract, the seller may perform the contract by delivering the goods but they are the wrong goods or in the wrong quantity or of inferior quality to that expected. In building contracts, big and small, there are snags: the floor area of a new factory may be 5% smaller than the specification agreed in the contract or a new kitchen in a house may have been fitted shoddily. These are examples of defective performance.

The second key to understanding breach of contract, therefore, is knowing what can be *done* about it: what remedies can be exercised and when?

REMEDIES

A number of steps must be considered in deciding the appropriate remedy.

Step (1): Contractual terms

There are a range of common law remedies which form part of the general law of contract but it is worth noting that the first place to look for the appropriate remedy is in the contract itself. The parties may have agreed in advance how breaches are to be dealt with. There are four main clauses attempting to deal with breach of contract which may be found in the contract itself:

(a) interest clause;

(b) limitation clause;

(c) exclusion clause; and

(d) definition of breach clause.

(a) Interest clause

Interest clauses are common in house purchase and sale contracts but are not restricted to those contracts. They apply to late payment of money and will stipulate that interest will run on any money due to be paid by the buyer to the seller if it is not paid on the due date of performance. A well-drafted clause will state the rate of interest and also set a time limit, after which the innocent party has the right to terminate the contract and seek other remedies if the money has still not been paid.

The Late Payment of Commercial Debts (Interest) Act 1998 implies interest clauses into business-to-business contracts and interest runs on late payment at rates fixed under that Act. Parties can contract out of this Act.

(b) Limitation clause

Limitation clauses attempt to cap liability for, among other things, breach of contract. (See Chapter 3 for a discussion of enforceability of these clauses and the applicability of UCTA to some limitation clauses.)

Another attempt to limit the cost for breach of *contract* is the use of liquidate damages clauses – common in building and construction contracts, under which the builders undertake to construct a building by a specified date. If this is not done by the agreed date of performance, then an agreed amount of money will be paid by them to the purchaser, usually on a weekly basis until the job is done and the obligation fulfilled. However, these clauses are not automatically enforceable, notwithstanding the fact that the parties have agreed their terms. The court will not enforce this type of damages clause if it is found to be punitive (ie a true penalty clause) rather than a fair assessment of likely losses. (*Lord Elphinstone* v *Monkland Iron & Coal Co Ltd* (1866); *Dingwall* v *Burnett* (1912); and *Clydebank Engineering and Shipbuilding* v *Castaneda* (1904).)

(c) Exclusion clause

The enforceability of clauses which try to avoid liability for breach of duty or breach of contract is discussed in Chapter 3. Exclusion clauses may or may not be enforceable.

(d) Definition of breach

The parties may try to agree in advance what they consider to be particularly important in the contract and to agree what would amount to a material breach of the contract. See below for the significance of materiality.

It should be noted that even if the contract does contain such terms, they may not be enforceable or they may not cover the breach in question and so it will then be necessary to look at the other remedies available.

Step (2): Sale of Goods

The second important issue to think about in considering a remedy is whether the Sale of Goods Act 1979 applies because this Act sets out remedies for breaches of those contracts. Although the Sale of Goods Act 1979 is often taught and examined separately from general contract law, a short discussion of its terms is necessary in this chapter (see below).

Step (3): Mutuality of contract

A party cannot seek a remedy for breach of contract by the other party if he is also in breach of the contract. Contract is a two-way bargain and so one party cannot insist that the other party fulfils his part of the bargain if he himself is in breach. Thus, in the case of *Graham & Co* v *United Turkey Red Co Ltd* (1922), an agent who breached his contract with his principal by selling rival goods could not insist that the principal, United Turkey Red Co Ltd, fulfil its obligation to pay him commission for the period that he was in breach. This is based on the principle of mutuality in contract law.

Step (4): Materiality

The remedy available will depend on whether the breach is "material" or not. In particular, the remedy of rescission is available only for material breach. A contract will have a wide range of obligations within it – some of which are more important or material than others. If the breach is of a minor obligation then it will not usually be considered material but if the breach is of an important part of the contract then the breach will usually be material.

- Refusal to perform is a repudiatory breach and is therefore material.
- Failure to perform any of it will be material. However, in the case of non-payment of money, it is probably safer to set a further deadline for payment which, if missed, will render the non-payment material (*Rodger Builders Ltd* v *Fawdry* (1950)).
- Failure to perform part of it or defective performance may or may not be material. For example, it is material to a contract for the hire of a car that the car provided (a) is available on the date agreed for collection by the hirer, and (b) has the required number of seats stipulated in the contract. It will not usually be material that the car is blue or red. It may be material that the car is a particular make and model or it may only be material that it falls into a class agreed between the parties. Consider the purpose of the car hire: a contract for the hire of a wedding car will be materially breached if the hire company substitutes a pick-up truck for the white limousine contracted for.
- The classic statement on materiality is found in *Wade* v *Waldon* (1909) at p 576 (per Lord Dunedin):

  "It is familiar law, and quite well settled by decision, that in any contract which contains multifarious stipulations there are some which go so to the root of the contract that a breach of those stipulations entitles the party pleading the breach to declare that the contract is at an end. There are others which do not go to the root of the contract, but which are part of the contract, and which would give rise, if broken, to an action of damages."

Step (5): Remedies

If there are no contractual remedies or statutory remedies available then the next step is to ascertain which remedies are available for each type of breach of contract.

Repudiation/anticipatory breach

If the contract is repudiated following the acceptance by the innocent party of the other party's refusal to perform the contract, then it is terminated. Therefore, the innocent party does not have to fulfil his obligations under it from that point on. Nor can he force the party in breach to fulfil his obligations under it as he has chosen the alternative path of terminating the contract.

However, he may have incurred certain costs in the period up to the date of termination through acceptance of repudiation. In our house buyer example, he may have booked a removal van and used the services of his solicitor in the legal work involved in examining the title deeds of the house etc. His remedy here would be to ask the court to award him *damages*. Damages is a monetary payment which the party in breach is obliged to pay to the innocent party and which represents actual loss arising as a consequence of that breach.

Anticipatory breach

If the refusal to perform takes place before the date of performance (rather than on it or after it) then the innocent party has a slightly longer menu of legal options to choose from. For example, if A and B enter into a contract whereby A will print adverts for B's business on 1 December 2005 and B tells A on 1 November 2005 that he does not intend to honour this contract and pay for the adverts, then that is an anticipatory breach on B's part. A has the following options:

(a) accept that refusal to perform and treat the contract as having been *repudiated* by B and treat the contract as terminated immediately on hearing of the anticipatory breach. A can then sue for *damages* for any losses incurred at that point; or

(b) A does not have to accept B's refusal to perform in November and can wait until 1 December 2005 and either:

  (i) perform the contract and force B to perform his part of the contract (ie in this case, payment of the contract price) or

  (ii) accept the refusal at that point and the contract is thereby repudiated: A could then go on to claim *damages*.

Authority for the point that the innocent party can refuse to accept repudiation and can perform his own part of the contract and then insist on performance by the party in anticipatory breach (or damages as an alternative) is provided by *White & Carter (Councils) Ltd* v *McGregor* (1962).

Late or non-performance

As discussed above, this type of breach does not mean that the party in breach has refused to perform (which is a positive action) but rather he simply has not done so. He may still perform his part of the contract but, at the very least, he will be late in so doing. The contract is therefore not repudiated but still "live". What can the innocent party do about that?

The innocent party has a number of options:

(a) remedies which can be taken without going to court:
   • retention;
   • lien;
   • rescission (material breach only);
(b) court-based claims:
   • damages (compensation instead of performance);
   • decrees for performance (actions for payment, specific implement and interdict).

Defective performance

The same remedies will be available as for late/non-performance but there are particular issues which may arise here:

(1) *Rescission*: rescission is available only for material breach and material breach is harder to establish in cases of defective performance than it is in a case of non-performance. For example, is it material that a newly built house has been fitted with electric storage heaters rather than gas central heating? The buyer may be furious but does that entitle him to rescind the contract and walk away without penalty?

(2) *Damages*: arguments about the measure of damages will be particularly relevant in cases of defective performance. How do we measure damages in this example? Is it the cost of replacing the heating system? What if the buyer decides that he wants to move in anyway and does not want the disruption of having the floors lifted for new pipework to go in etc and decides to live with the electric system but still wants some sort of compensation. Is that possible?

(3) *Sale of Goods Act 1979 remedies*: remember that these are available for sale of goods contracts.

Remedies explained (in alphabetical order)

Damages

Damages are the most widely available remedy. There is a checklist of requirements for a claim for damages:

(1) Is there a breach of contract? It may seem obvious but the innocent party must show that there has been a breach of contract and describe the nature of the breach. This will be obvious in a case of repudiation – the party in breach has refused to perform the contract and the innocent party has accepted that. However, note that it is *not* a prerequisite of a claim for damages that the breach be material (see above for definition of material breach).

(2) *Causation and remoteness.* It must be shown that this particular breach has *caused* loss or damage. This is more difficult. There must be a direct link between the breach and the loss or damage claimed. The loss or damage must not be too remote. For example, in the example of the house sale which has gone wrong, it is easy to imagine the repercussions of this for the innocent buyer who has been left without a house. He has run up removal van and solicitor bills. He may have to find alternative expensive accommodation at short notice because he has to move out of his own house or face a breach of contract claim from *his* buyers in a property chain. The expensive rented accommodation proves too far away to allow his son to walk to school as planned and he is sent by taxi every morning, which is costing a fortune. The innocent buyer then runs up more surveyor fees and solicitor fees in finding another property to buy. The tale of woe is endless. His wife is so depressed by the whole experience that she has to take 6 weeks off work without sick pay. How much of this is directly caused by the original breach? As far as the innocent party is concerned, all of it is directly attributable to the breach of contract. However, the courts take a stricter view. Note the following cases.

Hadley v *Baxendale* (1854)

This is the classic English case on remoteness of damage but is used as authority for Scots law too. The facts of the case are quite straightforward. The plaintiffs (the English term for "pursuers") owned a mill which was put out of action when a key piece of machinery, a crank shaft, broke. Production of flour stopped. The plaintiffs gave the broken shaft to a carrier to take to the manufacturer to use it as a template for making a new one. They did not tell the carrier that the new shaft was needed urgently, although the carriers did say that the shaft would be with the manufacturer in two days. Unfortunately, the carriers did not do their job well and delivery of the shaft was delayed. This delay amounted to a breach of contract on the part of the carriers. The question for the court to consider was whether the loss of profit which the plaintiffs experienced during this whole time was attributable to that breach or not. The court applied a two-part test:

(a) any loss arising as a natural consequence of the breach is covered by damages; and

(b) any special circumstances can be claimed for if the other party has been made aware of them at the time the contract is made.

On this basis, one would imagine that the loss of profits would fit neatly under part (a) of the test but, in actual fact, it was common practice for mills to have a spare shaft so that the mill would not come to a halt if one broke; so the court found that loss of production was not a normal consequence of late delivery of a broken shaft. Part (b) of the test did not apply because the plaintiffs had not made it clear to the carrier that they needed the shaft to be delivered urgently because it was crucial to getting production up and running again.

The difference between parts (a) and (b) of the test in *Hadley* was discussed in the following case.

Victoria Laundry (Windsor) Ltd v *Newman Industries Ltd* (1949)
A new boiler was ordered by the plaintiffs, who had a laundering business, with a view to expanding their business. It was delivered 20 weeks late, and the plaintiffs sought to recover damages in connection with the profits they had lost during the period when they should have had the boiler. The defendants knew the purpose for which the boiler was to be used and that it was required as soon as possible in order to grow the plaintiffs' business. The plaintiffs claimed under two headings: (a) in respect of new business valued at £16 per week; and (b) highly lucrative government dyeing contracts valued at £262 per week.

The court held that the plaintiffs could recover the loss of profits, including the additional profits for the new business, but not for (b), the special contract of which the defendants were not aware, and which they could not reasonably have foreseen.

Asquith LJ broke this rule down as follows:

"(2) In cases of breach of contract the aggrieved party is only entitled to recover such part of the loss actually resulting as was at the time of the contract reasonably foreseeable as liable to result from the breach.

(3) What was at that time reasonably foreseeable depends on the knowledge then possessed by the parties or, at all events, by the party who later commits the breach.

(4) For this purpose, knowledge "possessed" is of two kinds; one imputed, the other actual. Everyone, as a reasonable person, is

taken to know the "ordinary course of things" and consequently what loss is liable to result from a breach of contract in that ordinary course. This is the subject matter of the "first rule" [ie part (a) of the test] in *Hadley* v *Baxendale*. But to this knowledge, which the contract breaker is assumed to possess whether he actually possesses it or not, there may be added in a particular case knowledge which he actually possesses, of special circumstances outside "the ordinary course of things", of such a kind that a breach in those special circumstances would be liable to cause more loss. Such a case attracts the operation of the second rule [ie part (b) of the *Hadley* test] so as to make additional loss also recoverable." (1949) (at p 539).

In answering a problem question on remoteness, it is therefore necessary to consider (a) what sort of loss would be usual in the circumstances (whether the party in breach had thought about it or not) and (b) whether the party in breach actually knew of any special circumstances which would cause additional loss. In the house sale case, it is usual for someone left without a house to have to find alternative accommodation at short notice but not to have to send their child to school by taxi. On the other hand, if the seller actually knew that the reason the buyer wanted that particular house was so he could stop paying taxi fares then that might bring those costs under part (b) of the test. The question would certainly have to be asked so that all of the losses could be categorised properly in order for the tests then to be applied to them.

The extent to which "the ordinary course of things" can be taken was considered in the following case.

Balfour Beatty Construction (Scotland) Ltd v *Scottish Power plc* (1994)

This case centred on just how far the "ordinary course of things" can be deemed to have been known by the party in breach of contract. Here, the construction company Balfour Beatty contracted with the electricity supplier (then SSEB) to provide power to the company as it carried out a major piece of construction work. Power was lost at one point and this amounted to a breach of contract by the electricity supplier. As power had been lost, machinery had stopped and certain works had been suspended. Unfortunately, this included construction of an aqueduct, the construction of which required a continuous pour of concrete but which had been interrupted by the loss of power. This resulted in Balfour Beatty having to demolish what had been done before the power went off and rebuilding the aqueduct. The cost of this was over £200,000, which it wanted to claim in damages from the electricity supplier.

Was it foreseeable in the ordinary course of things that this loss would happen? Lord Jauncey of Tullichettle said that whilst it was "a matter of general knowledge" that concrete which had been poured would "ultimately harden", this general knowledge would not extend to knowing the "importance of the time involved in the hardening process, nor of the consequences of adding freshly poured concrete to that which had already hardened" (at 810F). The claim failed on the basis that it was too remote and not in the ordinary course of things.

What are contracting parties therefore assumed to know about the business of the other party, especially if they are not in the same trade or profession? Lord Jauncey said (at 810L): "It must always be a question of circumstances what one contracting party is presumed to know about the business activities of the other. No doubt, the simpler the activity of the one, the more readily can it be inferred that the other would have reasonable knowledge thereof."

(3) Quantification of loss or damage. Third, the actual amount of loss or damage must be quantified (punitive damages are not permitted under Scots law). How is loss to be calculated? Damages are there to "put the party whose rights have been violated in the same position, so far as money can do so, as if his rights had been observed" (per Asquith LJ in *Victoria Laundry (Windsor) Ltd* v *Newman Industries Ltd,* at 539). This merits discussion under two headings:

(a) _Patrimonial loss._ Patrimonial loss is financial or economic loss. In the case of the house sale which has fallen through, the buyer is left without a house, so to put him in the position he would have been in if the seller had not breached the contract, he should be the owner of a property worth the price of that house. However, the damages would not amount to the price of that house because he has not actually lost the money for it because he has not paid for it. On the other hand, the rent which he is paying on the flat which he has had to take at short notice is an actual quantifiable financial loss and the measure of damages is relatively easy there – the actual difference in these living costs.

Problems arise in measuring other losses and this has been considered in the case of two building contracts where the contract was not repudiated but the breach of contract was caused by defective performance. The cases are considered below.

Ruxley Electronics and Construction Ltd v *Forsyth* (1996)
Mr Forsyth contracted with Ruxley to build a swimming pool for him at home. Certain specifications were set out in the contract, including the

depth of the pool. Once it was finished, it was discovered that the pool was 6 feet deep rather than 7 feet and 6 inches as had been specified. Therefore, Ruxley was in breach of the contract. What was the loss? The breach did not render the pool useless and the change in depth did not adversely affect its end value because it was still safe for diving – the pool was just not as much "fun", in the words of Mr Forsyth (at 363).

One might argue that there was no loss at all and the courts have been restrictive in the past about awarding damages for distress or even for inconvenience. However, there *was* defective performance of the contract and if damages are designed to put the innocent party back in the position he would have been in if there had not been a breach then Mr Forsyth should have a deeper pool. How was that to be quantified in monetary terms (given that the action was for damages, not for rebuilding the pool)? The court had to decide whether damages should be calculated at the cost of rebuilding the pool (£21,650) or on a loss of amenity basis (£2,500) and left at that.

The House of Lords found that Mr Forsyth had contracted for a pool and that he had got one which he was happy to use. If they were also to award him damages at £21,650, he would have a pool *and* a large amount of money. He would therefore have received a substantial benefit and that is not the purpose of damages. Lord Lloyd of Berwick said (at 366): "... In building cases, the pecuniary loss is almost always measured in one of two ways; either the difference in value of the work done or the cost of reinstatement ... [but] ... it is not the only measure of damages." In this case, they awarded nominal or non-pecuniary damages (for loss of amenity) because they decided that awarding the usual reinstatement cost would be unreasonable and there was no difference in value to base the damages on.

McLaren Murdoch & Hamilton Ltd v *Abercromby Motor Group Ltd* (2002)
This Scottish case involved a claim against architects who admitted that they had breached their contract by being negligent in designing a heating system for car showrooms but denied that this had resulted in a loss or damage for the pursuers. Lord Drummond Young interpreted *Ruxley* to mean that "a pursuer will be entitled to the cost of making the works conform to contract except in two situations: firstly, where the cost involved is manifestly disproportionate to any benefit that will be obtained from it, in which case, the court should take notice of the disproportion; and secondly, where the defender leads evidence to show that there is a significant disproportion between the cost and the benefit ... [in which case] the court will be entitled to take a more critical view of the pursuer's actions."

(b) *Non-patrimonial loss and harm.* Non-patrimonial loss has been defined by the Scottish Law Commission as including loss of reputation, loss of amenity and loss of satisfaction at the contract not being carried out properly and non-patrimonial harm as including physical injury, illness, pain or suffering, distress or more severe psychological harm or trouble and inconvenience (SLC, *Report on Remedies for Breach of Contract*, No 174).

The general rule is that breach of contract claims cannot result in damages being paid out for mental distress. This general rule was set out in the English case of *Addis* v *Gramophone Co* (1909).

However, there are exceptions. Lord Denning held in the case of *Jarvis* v *Swans Tours* (1973) that a disappointing holiday which did not live up to the customer's expectations as based on the brochure could lead to damages for mental distress. He listed holiday contracts and contracts for entertainment and enjoyment as contracts for which damages could be paid out if breach resulted in mental distress.

Diesen v *Samson* (1971) is a Scottish case in which the court acknowledged that damages could be paid out for the loss and disappointment suffered by the bride and groom when the wedding photographer they had booked failed to turn up. Nominal damages were awarded in that case.

Farley v *Skinner* (2002) extended the exceptions (at least for English law) to the purchase of property which turned out to be on the flight path of Gatwick airport, even although the purchaser had specifically told his surveyor that he did not want to be on the flight path. The surveyor's breach of contract did not cause patrimonial loss as the purchaser had paid market value for the property, which took its location into account. He did not intend to move as he had bought the house as a retirement home. The surveyor argued that there was no loss so no damages could be paid out. The House of Lords disagreed and found that, although there was no patrimonial loss, the purchaser could receive damages for breach because this purchase fell into the category of contracts aimed at "procuring peace or pleasure" and, as the purchaser could not enjoy his property as he had hoped to do, he should receive damages.

Loss or damage suffered by third parties. As a third party is not a party to the contract, it is the general rule that loss or damage suffered by them as a result of a breach of that contract is not recoverable.

In measuring damages, therefore, it is important to know that loss can be a straightforward monetary loss which is then compensated or it can be more difficult to quantify as in cases of defective performance of contract. In the latter case, damages will usually be calculated by working out how much it would cost to put that right but the courts are also looking at issues of reasonableness in deciding if that is indeed the appropriate measure.

Restitutionary damages: the way forward? Damages are said to be compensatory in nature and designed to put the innocent party into the position he would have been in but for the breach of contract. Case law has limited damages to actual loss rather than extend them to cover payment for a thwarted expectation that the contract be honoured. However, recent English case law appears to suggest that a wider approach is starting to be taken in the measure of damages. The idea of restitutionary damages recognises that when a contract breaker has profited from his breach he should pay the innocent party not just for the innocent party's actual loss but also for part or all of the breaching party's gain. This has been applied in recent English case law: first, by the House of Lords, in *Attorney General* v *Blake* (2001); and, again, to some degree, in the recent case of *Experience Hendrix LL* v *PPX Enterprises Inc* (2003). The reaction of the Scottish courts is awaited.

(4) Mitigation. Fourth, the innocent party is not allowed to run up costs as a response to the breach and expect to be compensated for all of them, even if directly related to the breach. He must show that he has mitigated his loss. The thwarted house buyer mentioned above cannot book himself into a luxury hotel and stay there for 6 months without looking for a new home and expect that bill to be paid by the party in breach of contract. He must seek to minimise his loss but not at all costs – there is a requirement to take reasonable steps to minimise loss but no more than that (*Gunter & Co* v *Lauritzen* (1894)).

Decrees for performance

The innocent party may not want to terminate the contract. He entered into it for a purpose and he may want to force the party in breach to carry out his obligations under it (action for payment or specific implement) or to stop him from continuing in his breach (interdict).

Action for payment. Action for payment is suitable to recover a debt. If A performs a contract by installing a CD player in B's car and B does not pay the bill, then A can raise an action for payment in court to recover the debt.

Specific implement. This remedy is suitable for insisting on performance of an obligation other than the obligation to pay money. If B paid A to install a CD player in B's car and A did not do it then B could raise an action for specific implement to compel A to do it. Specific implement is a court order and wilful breach of this type of order is classed as contempt of court, which carries a potential jail sentence (maximum of 6 months under s 1(1) of the Law Reform (Miscellaneous Provisions) (Scotland) Act 1940).

Although it may seem to be a very simple and straightforward remedy, it is in fact subject to a number of important restrictions:

- It is not available to force performance of the contract if the breach is late or non-payment of money. The correct remedy for late or non-payment (subject to any contractual agreement to the contrary) is action for payment. The usual debt recovery procedures will be used.

- It is not available to enforce contracts with a strong personal element such as employment or partnership contracts.

- The courts will take into account the effect of the grant of the order on the party in breach and will not grant it if performance would actually be impossible or very difficult to enforce. The reason for this consideration must lie in the fact that the penalty for non-compliance is a criminal one. However, the case of *Retail Park Investments Ltd* v *Royal Bank of Scotland plc (No 2)* (1996) demonstrates that this exception will not be interpreted too broadly in favour of the party in breach. (MacQueen & Thomson, paras 6.8–6.9.)

Interdict. This remedy is suitable if A wants to stop B from doing something which puts B in breach of his contract. For example, interdicts are used to stop ex-employees who are in breach of the terms of restrictive covenants in their contracts with their former employers (see Chapter 3 for discussion of restrictive covenants).

Lien

A right of lien is a right in security and means that the innocent party can retain any property belonging to the party in breach until such time as the party in breach fulfils his obligations under the contract. Lien can be categorised as special lien and general lien. Special lien is the right to retain a particular piece of property until the breach is remedied; eg a TV repair shop can retain a mended TV until the bill for the repair is paid by the customer. General lien is the general right to retain property until breaches are remedied; eg solicitors have this right over their clients' papers, which can be retained until fees are paid.

Rescission

Rescission (or the right to rescind) is the innocent party's right to withdraw from the contract and not fulfil his obligations under it. The right to rescind the contract arises if (and only if) the breach is material. If the contract is rescinded then the contract is terminated. The decision to rescind the contract therefore rests with the innocent party. However, the innocent party needs to be very sure of his grounds before taking this step because any attempt to rescind a contract in response to a breach which is not material puts the "innocent" party in breach himself (*Wade* v *Waldon* (1909)).

The innocent party may or may not choose to go on to claim the further remedy of damages; but, if he wants to do so, he will have to raise a court action to obtain this additional remedy.

Frequently Asked Question

What is the difference between rescission and repudiation?
Rescission is the act of terminating the contract which is done by the innocent party in response to a material breach of contract by the other party. Thus rescission might be the response to a wide range of material breaches of the contract.

Repudiation is the *refusal* by one party to perform his obligations under the contract (a repudiatory breach), plus an acceptance of that repudiation by the innocent party. A refusal to perform is always material. This type of act can therefore be distinguished from other breaches such as failing to pay on time because it has at its core an actual *refusal* to perform rather than a mere *failure* to perform.

Further confusion arises when rescission is used by some writers to describe the response to repudiation. Repudiation is a material breach and so the act of accepting that refusal to perform is sometimes referred to as rescission – ie repudiation is met with rescission. Other writers keep the two concepts quite separate and define "repudiation" as "refusal to perform" plus "acceptance of that refusal".

The difference is very subtle and understanding it is not helped by the fact that different writers on the subject use the terms differently. This is acknowledged by Professor McBryde when he notes that the terms are used in a variety of ways (*Contract*, paras 20.02–20.05) as follows:

- Repudiation is sometimes used to mean anticipatory breach only.
- Some say that a material breach repudiates the contract.
- Some breaches are categorised as "repudiatory" (and others as material).

- Resiling is sometimes used to mean to "withdraw lawfully from the contract but not in response to a breach" of contract.
- Rescission is used in a number of different contexts: its correct use is as a non-court based remedy of termination of the contract by the innocent party in response to a material breach. However, the term is also used in cases of induced error and other problems with contract, and requires a court order (and should in those cases be called reduction)!

How is the student of law to make sense of this? If one takes the view that the term "repudiation" is limited to circumstances when there is a refusal to perform then that simplifies matters (*Edinburgh Grain Ltd* v *Marshall Food Group Ltd* (1999)). There is no need to rescind the contract in the case of repudiation because the contract is terminated by the conversion of the repudiation by acceptance. It may be argued that the innocent party's acceptance can be called rescission but the point remains that the contract is terminated by acceptance, whatever name is given to the action of the innocent party. The fact that the contract is terminated, whether by repudiation or rescission, allows the innocent party not to fulfil any further obligations under the contract but, in either case, he may still want to exercise a further remedy of damages (McBryde, para 20–30).

Retention
In this case, the innocent party does not terminate or cancel the contract but puts the performance of his own obligations under the contract on hold until the party in breach stops being in breach and the contract can get back on track. In other words, the innocent party decides to suspend his own obligations until the breach stops. For example, the most common method of retention is to withhold payment of the contract price (or some of it) until the goods are delivered or the services have been performed or a bad job has been corrected.

If the party allegedly in breach of the contract disagrees with the "innocent" party's interpretation of the breach (eg a common example is the argument that the performance is not actually defective) then the "innocent" party could actually be in breach and be sued for that money!

Specific remedies available under the Sale of Goods Act 1979
The Sale of Goods Act 1979 has certain inbuilt remedies in the following cases:

(a) breach of contract by the seller (s 15B);

(b) right of *partial* rejection by the buyer (s 35A);

(c) right to reject if wrong quantity delivered (if shortfall or excess is excessive) (s 30);

(d) unpaid seller's lien (s 39(1)); and

(e) unpaid seller's right to withhold further deliveries (s 39(2)).

(a) Remedies for breach of contract as respects Scotland: s 15B

"15B. – (1) Where in a contract of sale the seller is in breach of any term of the contract (express or implied), the buyer shall be entitled –

(a) to claim damages, and

(b) if the breach is material, to reject any goods delivered under the contract and treat it as repudiated.

(2) Where a contract of sale is a consumer contract then, for the purposes of subsection (1)(b) above, breach by the seller of any term (express or implied) –

(a) as to the quality of the goods or their fitness for a purpose,

(b) if the goods are, or are to be, sold by description, that the goods will correspond with the description,

(c) if the goods are, or are to be, sold by reference to a sample, that the bulk will correspond with the sample in quality,

shall be deemed to be a material breach.

(3) This section applies to Scotland only."

(b) Right of partial rejection: s 35A

"35A. – (1) If the buyer –

(a) has the right to reject the goods by reason of a breach on the part of the seller that affects some or all of them, but

(b) accepts some of the goods, including, where there are any goods unaffected by the breach, all such goods,

he does not by accepting them lose his right to reject the rest.

(2) In the case of a buyer having the right to reject an instalment of goods, subsection (1) above applies as if references to the goods were references to the goods comprised in the instalment.

(3) For the purposes of subsection (1) above, goods are affected by a breach if by reason of the breach they are not in conformity with the contract.

(4) This section applies unless a contrary intention appears in, or is to be implied from, the contract.

(c) Delivery of wrong quantity: s 30

"30. – (1) Where the seller delivers to the buyer a quantity of goods less than he contracted to sell, the buyer may reject them, but if the buyer accepts the goods so delivered he must pay for them at the contract rate.

(2) Where the seller delivers to the buyer a quantity of goods larger than he contracted to sell, the buyer may accept the goods included in the contract and reject the rest, or he may reject the whole.

...

(2D) Where the seller delivers a quantity of goods –

(a) less than he contracted to sell, the buyer shall not be entitled to reject the goods under subsection (1) above,

(b) larger than he contracted to sell, the buyer shall not be entitled to reject the whole under subsection (2) above, unless the shortfall or excess is material.

(3) Where the seller delivers to the buyer a quantity of goods larger than he contracted to sell and the buyer accepts the whole of the goods so delivered he must pay for them at the contract rate.

...

(5) This section is subject to any usage of trade, special agreement, or course of dealing between the parties."

(d) Unpaid seller's rights: s 39

"39. – (1) Subject to this and any other Act, notwithstanding that the property in the goods may have passed to the buyer, the unpaid seller of goods, as such, has by implication of law –

(a) a lien on the goods or right to retain them for the price while he is in possession of them;

(b) in case of the insolvency of the buyer, a right of stopping the goods in transit after he has parted with the possession of them;

(c) a right of re-sale as limited by this Act."

(e) Right to withhold further deliveries: s 39(2)

"39. – ... (2) Where the property in goods has not passed to the buyer, the unpaid seller has (in addition to his other remedies) a right of withholding delivery similar to and co-extensive with his rights of lien or retention and stoppage in transit where the property has passed to the buyer."

Title to sue

If a contract has been breached by one of the parties then who has title to sue for a remedy in the courts? The general rule is that only the parties to the contract have the right to go to court to enforce that contract or claim a remedy for breach of that contract. The following are exceptions to that general rule:

- a third party has *ius quaesitum tertio* (see Chapter 5);
- one party assigns (transfers) his interest in the contract to another party – the assignee then has title to sue for breach (see Chapter 5);
- the party who made the contract was acting for another (that party is therefore an agent of the principal and the principal has the right to enforce the contract) (see Chapter 5);
- the contract imposed burdens which run with the land (this is dealt with under property law);
- in some cases, a contract can be transferred to another party if the original party dies or becomes bankrupt.

Essential Facts

- A breach of contract is the failure to perform a contract in whole or in part. This allows the non-breaching party (or "innocent" or "aggrieved" party) to take certain action against the party in breach.

- There are three main categories of breach: repudiation/anticipatory breach, late (or non-) performance and defective performance.

- Repudiation is where one party tells the other that he does not intend to perform the contract. Note: some texts refer to *any* material breach as a repudiatory breach but the main point to know is that there is a difference between (a) actually refusing to fulfil the contract and (b) not getting around to performing it.

- Late (or non-) performance: the party in breach has not performed his obligations on time.

- Defective performance: the party in breach has fulfilled his part of the contract but not to the satisfaction of the other party.

- Remedies for breach of contract may be available to the innocent party provided he is not also in breach (mutuality of contract).

- Remedies can fall into the following categories: (1) contractual; (2) statutory (Sale of Goods Act 1979); (3) self-help; or (4) available through the courts.

- Contractual remedies include interest clauses, limitation clauses, exclusion clauses and definition of breach clauses. These will not be included in all contracts but if they are then they have to be considered first.

- Statutory remedies include rights of rejection, partial rejection and seller's lien under the Sale of Goods Act which applies to sale of goods contracts and will cover a great many contracts.

- Self-help remedies include retention (right of innocent party to withhold his performance, especially payment), lien (right to hold on to goods belonging to party in breach until breach remedied) and rescission (right to withdraw from the contract himself without penalty – available for material breaches only).

- Remedies available through the courts involve the innocent party raising an action in court for damages (monetary compensation for breach) or for a decree for performance (actions for payment of debt, specific implement (making party in breach perform) and interdict (stopping the party in breach from doing something) can be raised as appropriate).

- Repudiation: by accepting the other party's refusal to perform the contract, the innocent party can treat the contract as terminated. He may want to raise a court action for damages if he has incurred costs as a result of the contract.

- Late (or non-) performance: retention, lien, rescission, damages and decrees for performance may be available. Check any contractual and statutory remedies first.

- Defective performance: same remedies as for late or non-performance.

- Damages: most widely available remedy. Must show: (1) there is a breach; (2) it has caused the damages claimed for (causation); (3) quantification of that loss; and (4) mitigation of loss.

- Causation and Remoteness: apply *Hadley* v *Baxendale* test – the sum claimed must not be too remote from the breach. Any loss arising as a natural consequence of the breach is covered by damages and any special circumstances can be claimed for if the other party has been made aware of them at the time the contract is made.

- Quantification: patrimonial loss is financial or economic loss; and non-patrimonial loss or harm includes loss of reputation, amenity, satisfaction, physical and psychological harm. Patrimonial loss is easier to claim under damages but the courts do allow non-patrimonial claims in some circumstances (eg holiday contracts). Recent case law indicates that English courts may be moving towards restitutionary damages, which take a wider view of loss arising from breach.
- Mitigation – the innocent party must take reasonable steps to minimise his loss.

Essential Cases

Lord Elphinstone v Monkland Iron & Coal Co Ltd (1866): contractual limitation clauses such as liquidate damages clauses will be enforced only if they are a fair assessment of likely losses.

Graham & Co v United Turkey Red Co (1922): a party cannot seek a remedy for breach of contract by the other party if he is also in breach of the contract.

Wade v Waldon (1909): classic statement on materiality. Note: rescission available only if breach material.

White & Carter (Councils) Ltd v McGregor (1962): in a case of repudiation, the innocent party is not obliged to accept it and can therefore go on with his part of the contract.

Hadley v Baxendale (1854): the crank shaft damages case. Classic two-part test for causation and remoteness of damage: (a) loss naturally arising; and (b) loss for special circumstances if party in breach knew about them when contract made.

Victoria Laundry (Windsor) Ltd v Newman Industries (1949): damages case – further discussion of *Hadley* test and especially the difference between parts (a) and (b). Loss naturally arising includes things known about in the ordinary course of things but special circumstances must actually be known and not implied.

Balfour Beatty Construction (Scotland) Ltd v Scottish Power plc (1994): the cement case (damages); "ordinary course of things" did not include detailed knowledge of concrete pouring procedures.

Ruxley Electronics and Construction Ltd v Forsyth (1996): the swimming pool case (defective performance); innocent party could not receive both benefit of pool and cost of it so nominal damages paid out for lack of depth at one end.

McLaren Murdoch & Hamilton Ltd v Abercromby Motor Group Ltd (2002): car showroom case (defective performance); showroom built but heating system badly designed resulting in expensive heating bills. Courts will look at proportionality in assessing pursuer's claim.

Addis v Gramophone Co (1909): classic English authority ruling out damages for mental distress (since chipped away at).

Jarvis v Swans Tours (1973): disappointing holiday could result in damages for mental distress.

Diesen v Samson (1971): wedding photos ruined – damages awarded by Scottish court for loss and disappointment.

Farley v Skinner (2002): country house valued correctly but client had asked for "peaceful" retreat and it was ruined by flight path – damages could be awarded for loss of amenity even though no actual financial loss.

Gunter & Co v Lauritzen (1894): mitigation case – take reasonable steps to minimise loss.

Experience Hendrix LL v PPX Enterprises Inc (2003): English courts move towards restitutionary damages.

7 TERMINATION OF CONTRACT

When two parties enter into a contract, they do not usually expect it to last for ever. However, once made, it does subsist as a set of enforceable obligations until terminated and this chapter deals with the different ways in which a contract can be brought to an end. A contract can come to an end in a number of situations, as discussed below.

WITH REFERENCE TO THE TERMS OF THE CONTRACT ITSELF (NOTICE)

The contract may include a notice period, at the end of which the parties are freed from their obligations and the contract is terminated. Subject to employee protection laws, contracts of employment will usually terminate on one party giving the other written notice of, say, one month.

The contract may also be terminated through performance of the contract.

COMPENSATION

The Compensation Act 1592 allows one party to set off part of a debt owed by him to another against a debt owed by that party to him. If A owes B £100 and B owes A £30, then B can sue A for the difference.

CONFUSION

Very occasionally, the two parties to a contract will become one and that terminates the contract. If the debtor (ie the party to whom an obligation is owed) and the creditor (ie the party who owes that obligation) become one and the same party then the bilateral nature of the contract is extinguished and the contract is terminated.

DELEGATION

If A and B enter into a contract whereby A is obliged to do something under that contract, whether that is paying a price or carrying out another obligation, A's obligation under the contract can be terminated if another party, C, steps in and performs it for him. C can only do this if B consents but B cannot withhold that consent unless there is a particular reason why A has to perform himself. For example, if a student owed £1,000 in debt on a credit card, there could be no justification in the credit card company refusing to accept payment of that debt from the student's mother, unless, for example, the credit card company was prevented from accepting payment from third parties by law or banking rules. The mother's payment would extinguish the student's debt and the credit card company could not then claim the money from the student on the basis that his obligation continued because he had not performed it himself.

FRUSTRATION

There are certain situations in which the law recognises that a contract cannot be performed and, in those narrow cases, frees the parties from further performance. This should not be taken to mean that a party can automatically walk away from his obligations under a contract if he cannot perform them – a failure to pay a debt because one is short of cash is still breach of contract and *not* frustration. Frustration is limited to the following categories:

Supervening impossibility

Something may happen during the period between the date the contract was concluded and the due date of performance which makes it impossible to perform. This can arise in three situations:

Destruction of the subject matter (rei interitus)

This is illustrated in the case of *Taylor* v *Caldwell* (1863) in which a music hall had been hired for a particular date but unfortunately burned down before then. The court held that this frustrated the contract. There was no possibility of the owners of the hall being able to fulfil their obligations under that contract; they no longer had a music hall to hire out. It is, of course, possible for the parties to a contract to set out what should happen if the subject matter is destroyed; it is common for leases of commercial properties such as offices, factories and pubs to include clauses dealing with reinstatement of the building and which allow the contract to continue until the building is rebuilt. It should also be noted that where a suitable substitute is available then frustration will not operate to terminate the contract (for example, in a contract for a hire car, if one hire car is written off in an accident between the date of conclusion of contract and the hire period but another similar sized car is available then the contract of hire is not frustrated).

It is not necessary that the subject matter of the contract is actually totally destroyed; the law may imply destruction if it is not available for use for a reason that is beyond the control of the party in charge of it. This is called "constructive total destruction" and has been held to apply in a number of cases where there was no actual damage to the subject matter but it was nonetheless unavailable for the use intended by the contract. For example, in the case of *Mackeson* v *Boyd* (1942), a large house was to be let out under a contract. Unfortunately, war broke out and it was requisitioned for use by the authorities so not available for use by the tenants. Similarly, most contracts do not depend on one particular person performing them – if a customer contracts with a double glazing firm to put up a conservatory then it does not usually matter which team of workers is sent out from the firm to do the work and the fact that one of them has broken his leg and cannot work would not be enough to frustrate the contract. However, in contracts that do have an element of *delectus personae* (where it is important that the particular person (or persons) performs the contract) then injury to one may frustrate the contract. This is neatly demonstrated in the case of *Condor* v *Barron Knights* (1966) in which Condor contracted to perform as a drummer in a pop group. His duties were to play on every night of the week the group had an engagement. He fell ill and was told by doctors to restrict his performances to four nights of the week. The group terminated his contract. The court held that the contract was discharged by frustration. (NB employment contracts are now subject to extensive employment law). In a case of *persona delectus* (ie the identity of the other party is important) then the inability of that party to perform will frustrate the contract.

Supervening illegality

The law may be changed during the period between the date the contract is made and the due date for performance which makes it illegal. This would happen if war was declared and the contracting parties belonged to enemy states as in the case of *Fraser & Co Ltd* v *Denny, Mott & Dickson Ltd* (1944).

Supervening illegality can arise even in less drastic circumstances; for example, if a legal ban was placed on certain food additives then contracts already in place between the manufacturer and the retailer might be frustrated because it would become illegal for the manufacturer to supply food with that additive in it and for the retailer to sell that on to consumers. However, this would depend on whether the food could be supplied without the additive because if this ban simply meant that the food had to be made without it then the legislation might inconvenience the parties but it would not be enough to frustrate the contract.

Similarly, would a legal ban on smoking in public places frustrate a continuing contract between a pub landlord and a cigarette manufacturer made before such a ban? The landlord's market might be smaller as fewer people would buy the cigarettes in his premises if they had to smoke outside. However, provided the ban did not actually extend to prohibiting the sale of cigarettes then it could be argued that the ban did not frustrate the contract but merely affected the business conditions of the purchaser and that would not be enough under the law of frustration to terminate the obligations.

Supervening change in circumstances

A contract may still be frustrated even if it is not impossible or illegal to perform but events take a turn which means that the nature of the contract is changed and becomes something different from that contemplated by the parties when they made the contract. However, that would not extend to something simply becoming less profitable than hoped for. The application of this type of frustration is demonstrated in the following cases.

Krell v *Henry* (1903): Henry hired a flat from Krell in Pall Mall for two days. It was not stated in the contract that the purpose of the hire was to view the Coronation procession of Edward VII, but the letting was for the two days for which the Coronation was scheduled. The Coronation was postponed because of the King's illness, and Henry tried to cancel his contract with Krell who refused and sued him for the rent. The court held that the contract was for licence to use rooms for a particular purpose (implied condition since it was not express in the contract), and since the Coronation was postponed, the contract was frustrated. This decision was based on the court's findings that the whole point of the contract and the reason that it had been entered into by both of the parties was for the purpose of watching the Coronation. However, this case has been treated with reserve in later cases and so this type of frustration is very narrow.

What if the parties have already carried out some of their obligations before the contract is frustrated? If that has happened then there must be an accounting between the parties following frustration as in the case of *Cantiere San Rocco* v *Clyde Shipbuilding Co* (1923).

NOVATION

One contract will be terminated if the parties to it decide to replace it with a new agreement. So, for example, parties to a contract for the purchase and sale of bulk orders for tomatoes may renegotiate their terms of business and decide that delivery and payment will take place at different times from their previous arrangement. This new arrangement is a new contract and it replaces the old one. One party cannot then decide that the old contract was a better deal for him and resurrect it; it has been terminated through novation.

PRESCRIPTION (PRESCRIPTION AND LIMITATION (SCOTLAND) ACT 1973)

What happens if a long period of time passes after the contract is concluded without any action being taken to perform or enforce it? Does it last forever? The answer is no – the Prescription and Limitation (Scotland) Act 1973 places a time limit on how long certain obligations can last if no action is taken on them for a specified period of time. The relevant time period for contracts (unless specifically excluded under the Act) is called short negative prescription and lasts for 5 years. The effect of prescription means that if a contract is not subject to a "relevant claim" or "relevant acknowledgement" within that 5-year period, the obligations under it are extinguished.

A relevant claim would include one party trying to enforce the contract and relevant acknowledgement would include one party actually performing his obligations or writing to the other party making it clear that the obligations were still "live".

The excepted contracts are:

- contracts contained or evidenced in a probative writ (except cautionary obligations or those which contain an obligation to pay a periodical sum of money such as rent);
- partnership and agency contracts;
- contracts relating to land (except those requiring a periodical sum of money);
- imprescriptable obligations (this includes real rights of ownership in land and the right to challenge a contract on the grounds of invalidity *ex facie* or forgery).

Essential Facts

- Contracts can be terminated by compensation, confusion, delegation, frustration, novation and prescription.
- Frustration happens when there is supervening impossibility: destruction of the subject matter, supervening illegality or a supervening change in the circumstances. The obligations are extinguished.
- Prescription is regulated by the Prescription and Limitation (Scotland) Act 1973.

Essential Cases

Taylor v Caldwell (1863): music hall case; contract for hire of hall frustrated when it was burned down.

Mackeson v Boyd (1942): Tenancy frustrated when country house requisitioned in the war (constructive destruction of subject matter).

Condor v Barron Knights (1966): illness of drummer frustrated contract of employment (*delectus personae*).

Fraser & Co Ltd v Denny, Mott & Dickson (1944): supervening illegality caused by declaration of war.

Krell v Henry (1903): coronation case – purpose of contract thwarted when coronation postponed.

8 CROSS-BORDER CONTRACTS

If one party to a contract lives or does business in one country and the other lives or does business in another country, then problems of choice of law and jurisdiction can arise. Whose law and whose court system should determine disputes over validity, construction or breach of contract etc?

JURISDICTION

The first place to look is the Civil Jurisdiction and Judgments Act 1982 (as amended) which deals with the choice of *court* as between EU Member States and with issues of enforceability of judgments. This UK Act was first passed to implement the 1968 Brussels Convention on Jurisdiction and Enforcement of Judgments in Civil and Commercial Matters. It has been amended to take into account the new Council Regulation (44/2001) on Jurisdiction and the Recognition and Enforcement of Judgments in Civil and Commercial Disputes (the Brussels Regulation). These changes were then incorporated into the 1982 Act by secondary legislation, the Civil Jurisdiction and Judgments Order 2001 (SI 2001/3929).

The Brussels Regulation covers all EU countries other than Denmark which continues to follow the Brussels Convention, exercising her opt-out under Article 3 of the Protocol annexed to the Amsterdam Treaty.

Rules between EU countries and EFTA countries (Switzerland, Iceland and Norway) follow the 1988 Lugano Convention (which is similar to the Brussels Convention).

There are specific rules about jurisdiction for contract cases:

- General rule: disputes should be resolved in the courts of the country where the defender is domiciled or has a place of business.
- Special rules: disputes over matters relating to contract can also be resolved in the courts of the place of performance.
- Consumer contracts: businesses located in one European Member State which contract with consumers in another Member State (except Denmark) can be sued for breach of contract in the consumer's Member State. This depends on whether the business has pursued commerce there, which can take the form of marketing or even the use of a website to attract consumers from elsewhere in the European Union.

However, the applicable law may be different, in which case jurisdiction may change again.

CHOICE OF LAW

This decision will usually be made by reference to the Contracts (Applicable Law) Act 1990 which is a UK Act implementing the Rome Convention on the Law Applicable to Contractual Obligations 1980.

The rules

Article 3. The starting point for ascertaining the choice of law is to look at what the parties have agreed. Article 3.1 of the Rome Convention states: "A contract shall be governed by the law chosen by the parties. The choice must be express or demonstrated with reasonable certainty by the terms of the contract or the circumstances of the case. By their choice the parties can select the law applicable to the whole or a part only of the contract."

Article 4. If the choice of law has not been agreed then the rules in Article 4 must be brought into play. They are quite complex and the general and special presumptions for determining choice of law are subject to the rebuttal that the law of another country altogether can be chosen if there is evidence that it is actually more closely connected than the law which would apply under the presumptions. The relationship between the presumptions and this caveat has been the subject of much litigation and academic debate. The important point to note, however, is that the place of business of the performer of the main obligation under the contract rather than the place of performance of the contract is more important for choice of law, which contrasts with the position on choice of court.

Article 4.1 states: "To the extent that the law applicable to the contract has not been chosen in accordance with Article 3, the contract shall be governed by the law of the country with which it is most closely connected. Nevertheless, a severable part of the contract which has a closer connection with another country may by way of exception be governed by the law of that other country." A number of general presumptions will be applied to determine "most closely connected" but, of these, the place of business of the main performer of the contract at the time the contract was concluded has been held to be "crucial" in finding out which law governs the contract (*Caledonia Subsea Ltd v Mircoperi SRL, also known as Caledonia Subsea Ltd v Microperi Srl* (2002)).

However, a set of special presumptions may apply to certain contracts.

Contracts relating to immoveable property are covered by Article 4(3). Where the subject matter of the contract is a right in immoveable property (eg ownership of a house) or a right to use immoveable property then the country where that property is situated is presumed to be the country most closely connected with it.

Contracts for the carriage of goods are covered by Article 4(4). These contracts are not subject to Article 4(2). The country most closely connected for these contracts is the one which is the carrier's principal place of business and the place of loading or discharge or principal place of business of the consignor.

Article 4(5) allows for all of these rules to be disregarded if there is evidence that the contract is more closely associated with another country altogether: "Paragraph 2 [re general presumptions] shall not apply if the characteristic performance cannot be determined, and the presumptions in paragraphs 2, 3 [re immoveable property] and 4 [re carriage of goods] shall be disregarded if it appears from the circumstances as a whole that the contract is more closely connected with another country." This was considered in the case of *Definitely Maybe (Touring) Ltd* v *Marek Lieberberg Konzrtagen GmbH (No 2)* (2001) in which the band Oasis was contracted to perform in Germany. Their tour company sued the German company which had booked them for payment but the German company argued that they would not pay because a key member of Oasis, Noel Gallagher, had not performed with the band and so it was not the same group with which they had contracted. Was this to be decided under English or German law? The English court decided that it did not have jurisdiction because the terms of Article 4(5) pointed them to German law, notwithstanding that the place of business of the main performer of the contract (Oasis' tour company) was based in England.

Essential Facts

- Cross-border contracts have specific issues when it comes to considering where and under which legal system disputes should be heard.
- Jurisdiction: the Civil Jurisdiction and Judgments Act 1982 deals with the choice of *court* as between EU Member States and with issues of enforceability of judgments.

- Choice of law: usually made by reference to the Contracts (Applicable Law) Act 1990 which is a UK Act implementing the Rome Convention on the Law Applicable to Contractual Obligations 1980.

NOTE ON REFORM

The Scottish Parliament has legislative competence in matters of Scottish contract law and any future legislation will come from that Parliament.

ROLE OF THE SCOTTISH LAW COMMISSION

The Scottish Law Commission has kept the law of contract under review and has issued a number of reports, memorandums and discussion papers on certain aspects of contract law such as:

- *Remedies for Breach of Contract* (Discussion Paper No 109, April 1999);
- *Unfair Terms in Contracts* (Discussion Paper No 119, August 2002);
- *Defective Consent and Consequential Matters* (Memo).

Some of these reviews have suggested that reform is necessary and there is a strong argument for modernising the law of contract to codify and clarify the law rather than continuing to rely on judicial interpretation of principles and precedent. As yet, however, there has been no major overhaul of the Scottish law of contract.

EUROPEAN LAW

Much of our law on consumer protection has come from the European Union and many of these laws have a direct impact on contract law. For example, the Unfair Terms in Consumer Contracts Regulations 1999 were enacted in the UK to implement Directive EC/93/3; and the Consumer Protection (Distance Selling) Regulations 2000, which provide cancellation rights to consumers, are also a result of a European Directive (EC/97/7). It is likely that more consumer protection measures will be enacted in the future and students of contract must be aware of their impact on contract law.

The European Commission has also made moves to bring harmonisation of European contract law a step closer by publishing consultation documents in 2003 (Action Plan: A More Coherent European Contract Law) and 2004 (The Way Forward). Principles of European Contract Law (PECL) have also been issued. Unlike European Directives or Regulations, these Principles have no legal force in Scotland and do not have to be implemented. They may, however, influence development of the law and interpretation of it.

INTERNATIONAL LAW

Students of Scottish contract law should also be aware of the important role played by international law, particularly in matters of international trade.

GLOSSARY

Aggrieved party: if one party breaches the contract, then the other is said to be the aggrieved party (also known as the innocent party)

Breach: a breach of contract arises when one party does not perform his part of the deal or does it late or defectively

Capacity: the legal ability to enter into contracts

Consensus: agreement

Error: a misunderstanding or a misrepresentation of fact which occurs during pre-contractual negotiations or in the contract itself

Formality: the requirements for certain contracts which must be in writing

Frustration: an event which supervenes to terminate the contract

Innocent party: the same as "Aggrieved party"

***Ius quaesitum tertio*:** third party rights

Legality: a contract must not be illegal in law

Material: important

Offeror: a person who makes an offer

Offeree: a person to whom an offer is made

Personal bar: a party is prevented from enforcing his rights if he has placed himself in the position of not being entitled to do so in law

Personal rights: rights which accrue to a party under contract and which he can enforce against the other party to the contract

Promise: a unilateral gratuitous contract

Promisor: one who promises

Promisee: the party to whom the promise is made

Real rights: these rights differ from personal rights in that they can be enforced against the world (eg landowners have real rights over the ownership of their land and those real rights are registered in public registers)

Reduction (and "to reduce"): to have a contract set aside (either by consent or through court action)

Rescission: the right of an innocent party to terminate the contract in response to a breach by the other party (see Chapter 6)

***Restitutio in integrum*:** to put the parties back to their original position before the contract was concluded

Repudiation: the refusal by one party to perform the contract (see Chapter 6)

Resile: a legal method of withdrawing from a contract

Void: null; of no effect (see Chapter 6)

Voidable: a contract which is voidable is open to challenge on certain legal grounds and has effect up until the point that it is reduced (see Chapter 6)

FURTHER READING

Davidson and MacGregor, *Commercial Law in Scotland* (2003)
Huntley, *Contract, Cases and Materials* (2nd edn, 2003)
MacQueen and Thomson, *Contract Law in Scotland* (2000)
McBryde, *Contract* (2nd edn, 2001)
Marshall, *General Principles of Scots Law* (7th edn, 1999)
Woolman and Lake, *Contracts* (3rd edn, 2001)

INDEX